PRAISE FOR *WHEN GRIT ISN'T ENOUGH*

"For those who are serious about using education to serve as a vehicle for lifting people out of poverty, this book provides a sobering explanation of why it is so hard to do. Linda Nathan uses her many years of experience leading a successful urban high school to draw attention to the myriad of obstacles that so often thwart even the best-prepared and most ambitious students from achieving their goals. In doing so, she reminds us that it takes more than upbeat slogans and cheerleading to use education as a means to climb out of poverty. Insightful, revealing, and at times heart-wrenching, this book is an invaluable resource for those who hope to use education to transform the lives of our most vulnerable youth."

—PEDRO A. NOGUERA, PhD, author of *Excellence Through Equity*
and Distinguished Professor of Education, UCLA Graduate
School of Education and Information Studies

"*When Grit Isn't Enough* does a brilliant job of dismembering the prevailing fallacies about what makes for student success in higher education. Seamlessly weaving together stories and analysis, veteran educator Linda Nathan shows how, for poor, minority, and first-gen students, money (more precisely, the lack of money) and race do matter, and how it's fatuous to tell students on the cusp that, to make it, all they have to do is buckle down. *When Grit Isn't Enough* is both a powerful indictment of higher education and a blueprint for reform. If you read one book on education this season, make it this one."

—DAVID L. KIRP, Professor of the Graduate School,
University of California at Berkeley,
and contributing writer, *New York Times*

"It's a marvelous book, and badly needed at this time. Drawing on the powerful stories of children at the Boston Arts Academy, Linda Nathan bravely confronts the widely circulated myth that children who grow up in poverty can overcome inequity and every other daunting obstacle they face if they just 'believe,' 'persevere,' 'work like hell,' and show sufficient 'grit.' Many of these students do prevail, but Nathan makes it clear that 'grit' is not enough and that our adherence to this appeasing myth is letting a divided and bitterly unequal social order off the hook."

—JONATHAN KOZOL, author of *Savage Inequalities:
Children in America's Schools*

"In *When Grit Isn't Enough,* veteran educator Linda Nathan gives the lie to five popular but unproven beliefs about education that do little to improve schooling but instead blame the victims of poor and unequal schooling. This is a courageous book, one that challenges all of us, educators and non-educators alike, to do better for our most vulnerable students."

—SONIA NIETO, author of *Why We Teach Now* and professor emerita, Language, Literacy, and Culture, College of Education, University of Massachusetts, Amherst

"In *When Grit Isn't Enough*, Linda Nathan challenges deeply held beliefs like 'race and money don't matter' and 'if you just believe in yourself, then your college dreams will come true.' Through personal stories of alums of Nathan's school, along with extensive research, she argues that these assumptions *can* do harm. In this very readable book, she asks educators to confront the ethics of promoting these assumptions when other options, like high-quality career and technical education, can launch a low-income young person into a productive and enriched adulthood. A brave, honest, and optimistic book."

—NANCY HOFFMAN, cofounder, Pathways to Prosperity Network, and senior advisor, Jobs for the Future

"Storytelling can serve as a powerful tool for truth telling. Linda Nathan's *When Grit Isn't Enough* is truth telling at its best! Drawn on more than thirty years of teaching and leading in public education settings, Linda's stories show us, in no uncertain terms, how five long-held assumptions about American education are hurting thousands of talented urban students. Linda exposes us to painful truths and provides us with practical, implementable, and replicable solutions that can reverse these long-standing false assumptions. Most of all, she leaves us with hope, inspiration, and direction."

—JACKIE JENKINS-SCOTT, president emerita, Wheelock College, Boston

"In an age where we need courage far more than courtesy, Linda Nathan uses this book to do some much needed truth telling about schooling today. The American Dream that hard work will pay off is now a fallacy, and she shows us how and why."

—SARA GOLDRICK-RAB, professor of higher education policy and sociology at Temple University and author of *Paying the Price: College Costs, Financial Aid, and the Betrayal of the American Dream*

When Grit Isn't Enough

A HIGH SCHOOL PRINCIPAL
EXAMINES HOW
POVERTY AND INEQUALITY
THWART THE
COLLEGE-FOR-ALL PROMISE

Linda F. Nathan

BEACON PRESS, BOSTON

BEACON PRESS
Boston, Massachusetts
www.beacon.org

Beacon Press books
are published under the auspices of
the Unitarian Universalist Association of Congregations.

20 19 18   8 7 6 5 4 3 2

This book is printed on acid-free paper that meets the uncoated paper
ANSI/NISO specifications for permanence as revised in 1992.

Many names and other identifying characteristics of students and some
teachers have been changed to protect their identities.

Text design and composition by Kim Arney

Library of Congress Cataloging-in-Publication Data
Names: Nathan, Linda, author.
Title: When grit isn't enough : a high school principal examines how poverty
and inequality thwart the college-for-all promise / Linda Nathan.
Description: Boston, Massachusetts : Beacon Press, 2017. | Includes
bibliographical references.
Identifiers: LCCN 2017016606 (print) | LCCN 2017035694 (e-book) |
ISBN 9780807042991 (e-book) | ISBN 9780807042984 (hardback)
Subjects: LCSH: Universities and colleges—United States—Admission. |
College preparation programs—United States. | College dropouts—United
States—Prevention. | School-to-work transition—United States. |
Educational equalization—United States. | BISAC: EDUCATION / Secondary. |
EDUCATION / Higher. | EDUCATION / Educational Policy & Reform / General.
Classification: LCC LB2351.2 (e-book) | LCC LB2351.2 .N37 2017 (print) |
DDC 378.1/610973—dc23
LC record available at https://lccn.loc.gov/2017016606

CONTENTS

The Promise

It's lunchtime at the Boston Arts Academy and the cafeteria is bustling. In one corner, students show off their dance moves. At the opposite corner—as far away from the music as they can get—sit a group of about eight students hunched intently over sketchbooks as their conversations veer from the latest anime characters to the upcoming intersession course on fan fiction. Students at other tables engage in the more mundane tasks of eating, flirting, and checking homework. Lunch is the only time of day when the entire student body of about 440 is together, when students get some downtime to zone out for a few minutes away from the stresses of the school day—or their postgraduation plans. A number of seniors who can no longer put off those concerns make a beeline for the cramped office of BAA's college and career counselor, Ms. Hairston. They are determined to get a head start on college applications by taking advantage of Ms. Hairston's limited time and seemingly unlimited knowledge.

Students at BAA reflect the demographics of public high schools across the city of Boston.[1] About 40 percent are Latino, another 39 percent are African American, 16 percent are white, 3 percent are Asian American, and the remaining 2 percent identify as mixed/other or Native American. (Many Boston public high schools have many fewer white students.) Sixty percent are female and 40 percent are male, a breakdown similar to arts high schools throughout the United States.

Of the student population at BAA, 71 percent qualify for free or reduced lunch, which is the indicator for families living in poverty.[2] This figure is somewhat lower than the entire Boston Public Schools system, in which 78 percent of all students qualify. At BAA, 33 percent speak a language other than English at home, compared with 46 percent for the entire school system. Nearly 30 percent of Boston Public Schools students require specialized English-language learner (ELL) services, whereas only 6 percent of BAA students are registered for these services. Approximately 16 percent are students with identified special needs requiring instructional accommodations. This figure is somewhat higher for the school system at large.

In 1998, I became the founding headmaster of this specialized arts high school, where students audition in one of four majors (music, dance, theater, visual arts) for a coveted spot in the freshmen class. Each and every year that I was headmaster (until 2013), the students heard me say: "All of you will graduate from high school. And all of you will continue on to either college or a career." Perhaps I was trying to hypnotize them into self-actualizing this: after all, dropping out of high school is almost a one-way ticket to poverty, and I did not want any of my students to be part of that national statistic. Across the United States, only 59 percent of young black men and 65 percent of young Latino men graduate from high school in four years, compared with 80 percent of young white males.[3] The data for females of color in urban schools is a little better. Our high school graduation rate of about 85 percent is high compared with other urban high schools in Boston.[4]

There was a reason those seniors were hustling to Ms. Hairston's office that day: the Boston branch of the Posse Foundation was scheduled to announce its winners. In the Boston area, there are sixty Posse scholarships awarded annually. Over the years, on average, BAA seniors have received anywhere from one to four of the slots. Receiving a Posse means a four-year scholarship to a prestigious liberal arts college, as well as specialized and intensive advising, and a real posse, or support group, to meet with throughout all four years. Even students who may not at first be interested in attending the selected Posse schools still hope to compete for the coveted scholarships. Seniors know that if they are recommended and succeed in the first round of competitive group interviews, becoming a finalist, they have a chance of graduating from a good college without having to worry too much about money. They may have to worry about being far from home and one of the few poor or "minority" kids on campus, or about feeling completely out of place socially or culturally, but they will be on their way to a degree—and they will have their posse.

"When should we hear?" one young woman anxiously asks Ms. Hairston. "Didn't they say by noon today?" Marcia has been an honor roll student since arriving at BAA. She is a vocalist but much more interested in social and political issues than in a career as a professional musician. Without a full scholarship, college is not a possibility for Marcia. She knows this. She also knows that while her mother wants her to continue her education, her absence will make things difficult at home. Marcia has a disabled sister who requires full-time care. Her mother works nights, and Marcia and her stepfather share the responsibility of taking care of her sister in the evening. Marcia has juggled a lot during the last four years. She doesn't dare wish too hard for good news. Her best friend, Jayla, who is also competing for a Posse, squeezes her hand. "Come on," Jayla says, "let's stop checking our e-mail and get something to eat. By the time we come back, we'll hear something."

Ms. Hairston assures them both that if she gets the call or e-mail first, she will track them down. Three large room dividers carve out space in the guidance office surrounding Ms. Hairston's desk. Those dividers are covered with pictures of BAA graduates from the past sixteen years. Since 2000, Ms. Hairston has assured seniors that college was within their reach. For many, the promise has been fulfilled; for others, the challenges have been insurmountable.

FALSE PROMISES?

Since stepping down as BAA's headmaster, I have oftentimes wondered how well the school fulfilled my annual promise that "everyone will finish high school and go on to college or a career." For a long time our statistics have remained constant: 94 percent of our graduates are accepted to college or career training. On the surface, that number offers evidence in support of a great American assumption: everyone is equal. I can't imagine having said anything differently at those opening assemblies as

125 freshmen looked eagerly at me and anxiously at their peers, wondering if they would be the next star in their field. But with the benefit of time and space, I am troubled that I may have inadvertently perpetuated a falsehood. As I rejoice at the many hundreds of our successful alumni, I rage at the circumstances that reduce so many others to low-wage jobs. Many may be accepted to college, but how many finish? Acceptance is not the same as enrollment; of that 94 percent accepted, an average of 65 percent actually enroll. Of those who enroll, how many graduate? In various studies we did at BAA, we found that about two-thirds of our students finish with a degree. Some may say that this outcome is outstanding. How many urban schools can boast such college-completion rates? But I see it differently. What about the other one-third who do not get a degree? Where are they now? What were the barriers between them and college access or retention, and how could we have better prepared them to overcome those obstacles, or to find another path to success?

Shanita, whose story I related in my first book, *The Hardest Questions Aren't on the Test*, is one of the students for whom the promise proved false. Despite being the valedictorian of her class, she did not go on to college. For complicated reasons relating to a lack of experience or perhaps even shame, Shanita lost a scholarship because she didn't send in her deposit to hold her place. For years, Shanita's story has haunted me; in many respects it is the touchstone for this new book. It is not an individual story, but rather an iconic one—a story that is all too familiar to too many poor and black and brown young people. The deposit is a metaphor for the many invisible and visible obstacles that challenge or bar students' access. Shanita's experience propelled me to ask the central question in this book: How do schools, particularly under-resourced schools, best prepare our students for successful careers and/or college? Or, said differently, how do issues of access and equity shape our students' post–high school experiences? In this book I want to explore both students' success and challenges after high school and in college, and in addition, I want to better understand how we might prepare students for a career that may not include a four-year degree.

"College for all" is the new refrain. Many urban schools, starting at the elementary level, display the flags and banners of the teachers' alma maters along hallways and in classrooms. The idea is that if we surround young people with the possibilities of college then they will persevere and get there too. As the Pathways to Prosperity project of the Harvard Graduate School of Education found, as published in its 2011 report, "the lifetime earnings gap between those with a high school education and those with a college degree is now estimated to be nearly $1 million."[5] And the differential has been widening. In 2009 median earnings of workers with bachelor's degrees were 65 percent higher than those of high school graduates ($55,700 versus $33,800). We know the importance of improving college attendance and graduation rates for urban youth. In 2013, Barry Bluestone, political economist at Northeastern University, wrote that 80 percent of all US jobs in the life sciences will require a bachelor's degree or beyond.[6] In an earlier report, he stated that the "industrial sector in Massachusetts is neither disappearing nor dying, but rather it now has the technology prowess and efficiency to provide good and often exceptional employment for more than 260,000 workers well into the future."[7] According to reports such as Pathways to Prosperity, over 50 percent of these jobs do not require a bachelor's degree. Still, they require skills and training beyond a high school diploma. Between 2010 and 2020, 12 million of the 55 million US job openings (24 million new jobs and 33 million replacement jobs) will be filled by people with an associate's degree or occupational certificate.[8]

These statistics raise serious questions about the overarching ambitions of schooling as well as the role of those in education leadership. They also challenge educators to look critically at what must change if we are ever to embrace both vocational and career education as a serious undertaking in this country. In delving into these larger inquiries, I wanted to hear from students themselves. Students' lived experiences can provide a window through which to view urban education today, helping us to rethink the greater purposes of schooling with the goal of providing access to success for all.

CREATING FALSE ASSUMPTIONS

Alumni visiting BAA after college have recounted both successes and harrowing disappointments. Often when I shared their traumatic stories with colleagues outside the education field, I would be met by responses like "Well, maybe they weren't ready for college" or "Not everyone should go to college." I interpreted these responses as blaming the student rather than a system that is inherently unfair and inequitable. I wanted to understand more. As I stepped down from the position of headmaster and transitioned to a position at the district level (I remain on the BAA board), I decided to interview BAA alumni about their experiences post–high school. During the more than eighty interviews I conducted, similar words or phrases kept recurring in their stories. I distilled these ideas into a set of five beliefs or assumptions that frame both their successes and their failures.

1. Money doesn't have to be an obstacle
2. Race doesn't matter
3. Just work harder
4. There is a college for everyone/everyone can go to college
5. If you believe in yourself, your dreams will come true

I began to question these beliefs to better understand how they are perpetuated in our schools and society. First, I want to understand why these assumptions—which hold almost mythological power for Americans—are so prominent. What is their function? How do popular media substantiate or contradict these assumptions? And most important, who benefits from these beliefs?

Deeply held beliefs frequently go unchallenged in societies. They are how we explain phenomena or culture or history. They are often false; yet, they persist. I believe that these assumptions, or what I have come to call false promises, persist in public education because we hold so tightly to the American ideal of equality. It is this belief that I and many Americans desperately want to be true. It is this belief we fight for. But it is also this belief that we must fully unpack, deeply understand, and interrogate if we are to uphold our fragile democracy.

So many of my students' experiences in high school were about creating possibilities and hope. Our young people dove into academic and artistic debates because they were in an environment where the outcomes of their discussions mattered. They talked about capstone experiences that they had had (juries, exhibitions, performances, final papers, Senior Grant Projects) as some of the most engaging, stressful, and ultimately rewarding times of their lives. They spoke eloquently about art and community, and their roles in both. They saw that the adults around them—from custodial workers to administrative staff to teachers—had a stake in the well-being and success of the school. While there were certainly boundaries to decision making, everyone was encouraged to feel a strong sense of agency—that their opinions mattered. Regardless of social class, educational background, race, gender, sexual orientation, language background, or immigration status, everyone was a valued member of the community. Thus the young people were being prepared, on a daily basis, to participate in the complex world beyond school. That participation is, in fact, how we would measure our success—by our students taking up the mantle of artists, scholars, and active citizens. One senior wrote of her determination to do just that in the wake of Donald Trump's election. She sees Trump "as a man who took advantage of his privileges to belittle people who do not look or think like him." She states, "As a young woman of color who comes from a background that values people [regardless of] their immigration or socioeconomic status, I refuse to accept this. . . . If there is one thing that BAA has taught me, it has been that I do not have to limit myself. I *can* be an artist. I can be a scholar. I can be a citizen and most important, I *will* be an activist." She concludes that she plans to major in political science and run for office to ensure that BAA's shared values—passion with balance, vision with integrity, community with social responsibility, and diversity with respect—live on.

I recognize my own need to sustain the assumptions of equality and opportunity because I entered this profession to ensure that young people like this senior would be successful. And so many are. And those successes propel us further and allow us to stay hopeful.

But when I listened closely to those graduates who had not been successful, I became committed to more deeply understand their experiences. How can we inspire young people to reach for the stars while knowing the deck is stacked against them? What conclusions might I draw about the ways schools and policies need to change so that the environments I know are possible become a reality? Listening to my students' stories kept bringing me back to the question of democracy. Even those students who felt betrayed by false promises recalled feeling supported and empowered at BAA. I was determined to learn from those stories.

At the same time that I was interviewing BAA alumni, my own children were going off to college. The juxtaposition was often very stark. My three children all went to selective colleges and earned their degrees. There was never a question that they would attend college and graduate. They may have experienced some adjustment difficulties, socially and even academically, but their job was clear: earn a diploma. They never suffered racism or fear of how to pay for lodging, food, books, or classes. When they were frustrated with how to navigate the student health system or any other college support, they had two college-educated parents to turn to with questions. When they wanted to know about study abroad, for example, and found the college information sessions confusing, they just called home. They also didn't have to worry about how to pay for that experience. The path to their success was made smooth by the supports of a middle-class background. It is certainly possible to succeed without those supports. But I wondered just how many more of our students would have attained college degrees if they were as free to focus on their studies as my kids had been.

QUESTIONING HOW WE ATTAIN SUCCESS

Taken together, the five assumptions listed above can be dangerous because they reinforce the deeply held American belief that success is individually created and sustained. "If I could do it, so can you" is an echo of the "just work harder" assumption. It is the "pull yourself up by your bootstraps" ethos to which so many generations of Americans adhere. Yet data repeatedly show how poverty, social class, race, and parents' educational attainment more directly influence an individual's success and potential earnings than any individual effort. We clearly do not yet have a level playing field, but this belief is all but impossible to challenge. Whenever we hear of another bootstraps story, we want to generalize. We disregard the fact that luck often plays a major role. And in generalizing and celebrating the individual nature of success, we disregard the imperative to rethink social and economic policies that leave many behind.

Diane Guerrero, author of the 2016 memoir *In the Country We Love*,[9] is one of BAA's most famous alumni. If anyone embodies the bootstraps ethos, it is she. In her memoir Diane, who graduated in 2004, tells the heartbreaking story of being a child of undocumented parents who were eventually deported. Diane went to live with the family of a friend from BAA. She worked pretty much full-time throughout high school to pay for her expenses. She rarely missed a day of school and made honor roll or high honors for all four years.

Today Diane is a spokesperson for immigration reform and a much loved actress who plays Martiza in *Orange Is the New Black*, the Netflix series about a women's prison. She won the 2017 SAG award for Best Latina Actress. Diane embodies the assumption: "If you believe in yourself, your dreams will come true." Yet she reminds me that you still have to get up every morning and audition. "Nothing is handed to you. This is hard work."

While I celebrate Diane, and so many like her, I wrote this book to expose how, in many cases, hard work is just not enough. I have too many students who, despite their best efforts, have not been able to graduate from college. I have too many students who because of misreading a form, or experiencing a family tragedy, or because of racism or lack of explicit support from their college ended up leaving and owing money for a degree they never got.

As one young alumna told me, "I never thought BAA was about all of us becoming professional artists, but rather the opportunity to pursue that if we wanted. But I knew that BAA was a place to learn about appreciating the world, one another, and all of our differences. I think that we knew we were special and so we shouldn't fall into those traps or stereotypes everyone has about 'inner city kids' 'getting pregnant or not having jobs.'" This book is an attempt to learn from the stories of these young people, and the hopes they have for their own lives.

Finally, this book posits that if we do not educate all of our students to high levels, we endanger our democracy. Schooling and education hold out the promise of a robust democracy. However, if we are regularly denying access to a certain segment of our population, specifically poor and people of color, how can our democratic structures survive?

The examination of these assumptions through the stories of the Boston Arts Academy graduates may help us better understand how our systems must change and how we must work differently both in pre-K–12 and higher education. Think about what it means to peg your hopes on one full-tuition scholarship for college, as Marcia and Jayla did with the Posse scholarship. The access and support it promises can easily make the difference between going to college or not, and graduating from college or not. But this opportunity is limited to a chosen few. If we believe that everyone in America has the right to a fulfilled life, and that access to quality higher education is essential to accessing that life, we owe it to our young people to implement change.

CHAPTER ONE

"Money Doesn't Have to Be an Obstacle"

Americans tend to believe in meritocracy: if you are smart and a go-getter, you'll be successful. But it doesn't always work that way. Plenty of smart, hardworking students are accepted to college, but fewer en-roll, and many of those don't graduate. To drill down a little further, we need to take a look at persistence. College persistence rates are measured by looking at the number of students who return to that same institu-tion after their first year. BAA graduates' persistence rate for 2013 was 83.9 percent. Boston Public Schools' was 84.1 percent (including exam schools, the three schools in the Boston Public Schools system for which students take an academic entrance test and are admitted based on their scores), and the national persistence rate was 58.2 percent.[1]

In an earlier BAA college-retention study (2008), 63 percent of BAA graduates had either finished college within six years or were still pursu-ing higher education. The average national rate for college graduation with a bachelor's degree within six years hovers around 53 percent, and is much lower for students of color or from low socioeconomic back-grounds. The data is worse for community college students, with 39 per-cent obtaining a credential from a two- or four-year institution within six years.[2] This chapter and the following will examine some of the major factors that keep students from enrolling or persisting in college, who is responsible, and what we can do to help.

Everyone knows money is important. For those privileged to have enough of it, money is not an obstacle for living a decent life or for college access. My husband and I frequently say, "Money isn't everything," but only the freedom of *having* money allows us to say such a thing. We didn't want our own children restricted in their college choices. Of course, we hoped that they would consider attending Tufts University, where my husband is a professor, so that, if admitted, they would be eligible for tuition remission. But we didn't want to limit their explorations or plans. Many of my friends will espouse similar statements: "We will take out loans if we have to" or, "I'll be working to pay this tuition off for another twenty years." Many of our friends began a college fund when their children were born. I know of many families who enlist the help of a grandparent to pay for a grandchild's tuition. So, for the children of the "haves," the cost of college is a consideration, perhaps, but it doesn't predetermine the future.

However, within the urban public school arena where I have worked for four decades, the assumption that "money isn't everything" is patently false. At BAA, we hope our students will receive adequate scholarships or federal loans. We urge students to go to state colleges and universities where tuition might be more affordable. We counsel kids against taking on too much debt. But no matter what approach we take, cost is a huge obstacle in accessing quality higher education. A recent study reports that state funding for higher education has fallen by 18 percent since 2008.[3] Money, or the lack of it, can easily determine the kind of future a young person will have. Some families have the good fortune to assume that no matter the monetary demands, college is accessible. But that is just not true if you are poor or don't have the social or cultural capital to navigate the system of higher education. The data is incontrovertible: elite colleges and flagship colleges enroll more students from the top 1 percent of the income bracket than the bottom half of the income distribution.[4]

A recent analysis by the American Council on Education notes that fewer low-income graduates are enrolling in college even though student aid from federal and institutional sources has increased since 2008.[5] At that time, 55.9 percent of low-income high school graduates enrolled in college. By 2013, that figure had dropped to 45.5 percent. The study offers a possible theory to explain this data. "The rapid price increases in recent years, especially in the public college sector, may have led many students—particularly low-income students—to think that college is out of reach financially." The trends are particularly worrisome in light of the fact that as "the percentage of low-income students in elementary and secondary schools is increasing, the percentage of low-income students who go on to college is falling." And, as stated above, funding for state colleges has decreased dramatically.

Educators must help young people dream big, but we have to confront the fact that the dreams of the economic have-nots are not just deferred but can be obliterated for lack of access to economic capital. Furthermore, we need to better understand the fragility that poverty creates. In the stories I recount in this chapter, some students made avoidable errors that derailed their college plans. However, if these students had come from upper-middle or even middle-class households, where conversations about college are constant and where a safety net protects them from falling too hard after a misstep, I don't believe these errors would have had such a devastating effect. It is easy to point fingers and blame the individual student: how could he/she have made that mistake? My point here is not to blame the individual but rather to examine the webs of inequity that can entrap young people, especially those living in poverty. Furthermore, we have so idealized individual stories of success that they have achieved folklore status for young people. Think about the ways in which we celebrate pull-yourself-up-by-the-bootstraps celebrities like Jennifer Lopez or Jay Z. These performers are household names among young people, and role models for those growing up in impoverished neighborhoods. While I am enormously proud of BAA success stories like Diane Guerrero, they too obscure how the systemic issues of poverty and inequality can disable college access.

RAUL: THE SCHOLARSHIP ISN'T EVERYTHING

I remember when Raul bounded into the office, practically leaping over the high counter separating the sitting area from the secretary's desk, and came rushing through my door. "Wait a minute!" the secretary called after him as he flew past her.

"I got in! I got in!" Raul's voice cracked with emotion and a broad smile spread across his face. As he waved the letter in front of me, I managed to see that it was an early-admissions decision to a four-year college out of state. "And I got money. A full-tuition scholarship!" He thrust the letter into my hands and collapsed into a chair, his dark eyes filling with tears. Tears of joy. Tears of disbelief. As I read the letter, Raul kept repeating, "I didn't dare to dream that this could happen. I didn't dare to dream that I could actually get money for college! But I did! And I can go!! I can really go!"

I got up to hug him and agreed, "Of course you are going. You've worked hard for this. And you deserve it!"

Raul would be the first in his family to go to college. He comes from a large Dominican family and he and his sister, Raquel, are the first to have graduated high school. At graduation, Raul chatted excitedly about his plans to move out of state. He'd had lots of conversations with our guidance counselor about not taking out too many loans, but I was worried about where he was going to live. He assured me that if necessary, he could stay with a brother of his, whose house was close to campus.

A few weeks after graduation, Raul and Raquel visited BAA after going shopping at Bed Bath & Beyond for his dorm room supplies. They excitedly showed me their checklist. "We didn't get everything," Raul said. "I have hangers and stuff like that at home. But I didn't know I'd need a lamp."

Raquel grinned in agreement. "And I think he'll fall off his bed. We had to get these weird bed things—I think they call them risers. Everyone says it's the only way you have storage. Under your bed. But who puts their bed on blocks?!" Raul pulled the blocks out of the bag to show me.

I remembered buying those same risers when my eldest son went off to college. I also remembered being stunned at the long list of "must haves" on the dorm room list—everything from power strips to pillows. I recall as well the cost of all those items. But the popular media perpetuates a rosy picture of a first-year student's move into the dorms: luggage in all sizes and shapes, crowded hallways, choosing the bed if you get there first, and emotional good-byes with parents. My students also want to participate in this idealized experience. Buying the matching sheets and comforter is a statement that they too belong.

The next time I heard from Raul was in late February when he came to see me at BAA. "Why aren't you in school?" I asked. He looked despondent. "No money for housing."

As we retraced what had transpired in the previous eight months, I was haunted by the all-too-familiar story. Even though I have spent years working with low-income students like Raul, I fear I was incredulous when I asked him, "But hadn't you known that there would be a cost to housing?" Raul responded sincerely, "No, I assumed it was covered. They never told me." I tried again. "But you saw that there was a fee for housing? It was on the paperwork you got, right?" "I guess so, but I knew they had given me a scholarship," Raul explained. "I thought the bill was just showing what it would cost if I hadn't had the scholarship."

I tried a different approach. "Had you gotten any notice about your roommate or anything about which dorm you'd be living in?" Raul answered earnestly, "No. And that worried me. Other friends were getting their roommates and getting to know them on Facebook. So about two weeks before school started, I did try calling, but I was on hold for so long that I hung up. I tried later that week and left a message, but when I didn't hear back, I just assumed everything was okay. So I just went. I had received all the orientation memos and so I went on the day they said. I figured that since they gave me all those details in the memos, they wanted me. My mother told me that I could live with my brother if something didn't work out. He's in New Jersey too."

Raul's brother picked him up in Newark and they wound through farmland and countryside for about two hours before arriving on campus. Not until that drive did Raul realize how far away his brother actually lived from the school. His laser focus on the acceptance hadn't allowed for any consideration of logistical impediments. In getting into college, he had leaped over an enormous hurdle. Getting the full-tuition scholarship had been almost beyond his dreams. What could go wrong?

Raul described arriving at school with his luggage and new pillows. It was during registration that first day that he learned that in order to move into the dorm he needed to pay $14,000. "What was I supposed to do? I'd registered for classes—art, French, writing, neuroscience, and seminar. I was a freshman in college! Nothing was going to stop me." So, in the moment, standing in line at the bursar's office, he and his brother took out a loan so that Raul could start his freshman year. By the end of the first semester he was home—depressed, ashamed, and angry. "I would never have put myself in this situation if I had understood the scholarship didn't cover everything."

This moment marked Raul's mistake. The flaws in his thinking are evident to anyone who understands something about loans and debt, and is accustomed to reading the small print on documents. But knowing how far Raul had traveled literally and figuratively, I also understand why he would have signed those documents. Raul was not going to let college slip through his fingers. Although he was not adequately informed about what he was agreeing to, he could not concede that money was an obstacle to his plans. He had his matching sheets and comforter; he'd done his pre-orientation freshman reading! It's not that colleges are trying to pull a fast one on kids, but I can see how it feels like false advertising from the perspective of a senior in high school. He had received his acceptance letter, his scholarship, and even his orientation packet. What else was needed? It's also easy to lay blame on high school guidance counselors, advisors, teachers, or administrators. I continue to second-guess myself about what we could have done to prevent Raul's experience from being so debilitating. Our guidance counselor had warned him about looking closely at his housing options. But she had 100 seniors she was working with and another 125 juniors clamoring for attention. (And I should add that at BAA the guidance counselor to student ratio is quite good. Many urban schools have a single counselor for over 300 students.) Raul's faculty advisor, perhaps, could have asked more pointed questions as well. (All full-time teachers at BAA are advisors to a small group of about fifteen students in grades nine through twelve. Advisors are charged with helping their advisees navigate high school and beyond. It is our attempt to lessen the burden on the sole guidance counselor so that there are more adults involved in a student's academic, socioemotional, and artistic growth.) We can all rebuke ourselves for what we might have done differently, but the point of this story is not really about blame; rather, it is a chance to look deeply at the complex web of higher education. There is so much about the college process—application, acceptance, and preparation—that can be indecipherable to students who lack family members familiar with the experience or counselors with the time and resources to guide them every step of the way.

Raul, like so many students who live in poverty, did not have the social, economic, or even cultural capital to recognize the long-term financial implications of his decisions. How does a young man like Raul—honor roll, civic-minded, caring and charismatic, recipient of a full-tuition scholarship—end up serving frozen yogurt at Pinkberry? How will he ever pay back this loan? He insists, "I'm not going to be another statistic! Another Hispanic without a college degree. That isn't me!" What are our solutions? And what can high schools across America that are filled with young people like Raul learn from this awful experience?

This particular story shows that the habits and values we as educators had instilled in Raul, and that we believed were sufficient in ensuring his success beyond high school, weren't enough. We promise our graduates that our diploma assures them entrée into a career or higher education. We promise that our curriculum, carefully evaluated and recalibrated each year, and our three-pronged support system of arts, academics, and wellness, will assure their achievement after BAA. However, it is clear that high schools in urban America that are committed to college access and retention must do more than provide a high-quality education. We must begin to think about providing courses or modules on subjects such as student loan and debts. I wish that colleges felt it was *their* responsibility as well to ensure success for first-generation students, but as we will encounter again later in this chapter, far too many young people are forced to figure it out themselves. Unfortunately for so many disadvantaged people across this country, money *is* an obstacle. Money can mean everything in terms of how you survive in college and how you survive afterwards. Money can mean everything in terms of how much debt you can assume and how that debt impacts your life moving forward. As one student said to me, "College isn't set up for poor people."

THE REAL COST OF COLLEGE

I often found myself telling my students, "You have to go where you get the most money, even if that school isn't your top choice" (although, as mentioned, my own children didn't get this advice; while we hoped they'd take advantage of tuition remission at the college where their father taught, they were not limited to that option). When the much-touted John and Abigail Adams Scholarship was introduced in Massachusetts, promising free in-state tuition to students with high MCAS scores, I found it difficult not to champion that opportunity. However, the scholarship—like Raul's—does not cover as much as you might expect. In fact, as with many state schools, tuition at the University of Massachusetts now accounts for only one-third of the cost of going to college. In-state tuition and fees (in 2015–16 dollars) are $14,596. Room costs are $6,061, and a full meal plan is $5,320. Books are approximately $1,000. Health insurance is $2,200. Other living expenses are calculated between $700 and $1,400 per academic year.[6] The Adams Scholarship thus covers only about 11 percent of the total costs. Once you add all these items together, a student may be looking at a $14,000–$20,000 loan per year! How many kids understand what those loans actually mean? And if your grades slip in college and you lose financial aid or scholarships, you can be trapped forever, paying off loans and with no degree to show for it.

That is exactly what happened to Ashley. She went to a private college in Boston, on a full-tuition scholarship. But most tuition scholarships are a combination of institutional support and federal financial aid, which includes loans, and most scholarships are tied to maintaining a certain grade point average (GPA). In Ashley's case it was a 2.8. However, after her first semester, Ashley had a 2.5. She had gone to college with every intention of majoring in biology. She had excelled at science in high school and had interned in hospitals and research labs in the summers. She signed up for an introductory biology course as well as chemistry in her first semester. She soon found the workload overwhelming and dropped the chemistry class. Even with the lighter load, and going to office hours and tutorials on a weekly basis, she got a C- in biology. Her other grades suffered as well (another C- and a D+), but her advisor said that he thought she could pull through the next semester, and everyone told her she would eventually adjust to the rigors of college life. In fact, many of Ashley's friends were having similar difficulties. Ashley was determined not to give up. She and her two friends formed a study group. They promised each other that everyone would do well together.

Unfortunately, at midterms none of their grades had improved. The two friends, since they were not on scholarship, decided to drop the course and retake it in the summer. Ashley didn't have that option: her scholarship did not cover summer courses. She would have to pass, and with a good grade. However, she didn't get the C+ she had hoped for and her GPA dipped to 2.5. She lost her scholarship. She couldn't take out any more loans.

Given the opportunity, students from even the most competitive colleges might choose to take a particularly challenging class, like organic chemistry, for example, during summer school instead of the regular academic year. These students know that they'll have a better shot of making the grade if they're able to devote all their energies to this one tough course. I wonder what would happen if scholarship students could also take advantage of this "end-run." Ashley didn't have the economic means to access this well-documented route to success. She had no options, and no second chances.

When I last saw Ashley she was discouraged and angry. And she was still paying off her loans. She will be paying off her loans for years. She is working in a coffee shop in the evenings and trying to get a job in a hospital to satisfy her passion for lab work. "My friends from college are all working in labs. They tried to help me for a while, but, you know, we drifted apart. They don't have to worry as much about money as I do. They come from families where there is more financial support. But I had that scholarship and that was it. For a long time I thought I could go back, and I wanted to just beg them to give me another chance. But, you know, I began to feel that I didn't belong there anymore. Maybe I wasn't smart enough for college." I wanted to grab Ashley and proclaim that, yes, of course she was smart enough for college. But I couldn't erase those loans. Her dream of a college degree was evaporating. In order to return to college, she would first need to get her transcript released. But if you haven't paid the bill, you can't get the credits. For Ashley, there was no money coming from anywhere. She couldn't see starting all over again somewhere else. She would always have those debts weighing her down. I tried to keep in touch with Ashley for a number of years. I encouraged her to consider a state college where the costs would be more manageable. But after a while, she stopped responding. I think it pained her to hear my suggestions. She is living her reality now and it is not the one she had hoped for.

Articles abound discussing the perils of the college-debt crisis. In one, a 2013 piece by the Nobel Prize–winning economist Joseph Stiglitz titled "Student Debt and the Crushing of the American Dream," he writes:

> According to the Federal Reserve Bank of New York, almost 13 percent of student-loan borrowers of all ages owe more than $50,000, and nearly 4 percent owe more than $100,000. These debts are beyond students' ability to repay (especially in our nearly jobless recovery); this is demonstrated by the fact that delinquency and default rates are soaring. Some 17 percent of student-loan borrowers were 90 days or more behind in payments at the end of 2012. When only those in repayment were counted—in other words, not including borrowers who were in loan deferment or forbearance—more than 30 percent were 90 days or more behind. For federal loans taken out in the 2009 fiscal year, three-year default rates exceeded 13 percent.[7]

A student quoted in a 2014 article by *Forbes* staff writer Maggie McGrath said he was "surviving, but barely," and was wondering, "'Was college a waste?'"[8] But this is a question that BAA students wouldn't think to ask. They are encouraged, even graded, on their ability to pursue college or career choices after high school.

Carissa's story is similar to Ashley's. Carissa went to school out of state—to her dream college. She left after one and a half years because her financial aid didn't come through. "I can't blame my mother, but I really do. She didn't understand the system in this country. She came here when she was fifteen. She didn't understand that you have to do the FAFSA [Free Application for Federal Student Aid] and the forms every year. She kept telling me to take care of it. But I didn't have her tax forms. And she's working two jobs and has been helping me so much. I assumed she had done everything." Telling her story, Carissa is visibly upset, her voice shaking. "Suddenly, it was the middle of the semester of my sophomore year, and I got an e-mail—an *e-mail*—saying I couldn't go back to class. It was awful. I was so embarrassed. I didn't know what to do." I wanted to know if she had gone to speak to the people in the financial aid office. Carissa looked at me blankly. "Of course I went to financial aid. I had been going all the time to financial aid. I had been trying to explain that I would go home at Thanksgiving and get my mom to fill out the forms. But they said they couldn't wait." She takes a deep breath, then continues. "And then the financial aid lady said the worst thing to me. Just the worst thing." What was that? I asked. "She looked at my sneakers and my jacket and she actually said, 'I don't know how you can need financial aid if you can buy those nice clothes and shoes.' I just left. I didn't know what to think."

Carissa returned home and worked in the not-for-profit sector for three years with the Boston-based organization Citizen Schools. She was making $16 an hour from 12 to 5 p.m. every day. She also had a weekend job in a clothing store. "I'm taking a course at Northeastern that my job helped pay for, but in order for me to transfer, I have to figure out how to pay back my loans and I can't do that and go to school. Something had to suffer. It's been school." Carissa begins to cry. "I was going to be the first in my family to graduate from college. I still struggle with what I would have done differently. I didn't want to go to community college. I knew that was cheaper, but I was good at theater. I wanted to go where I could really get training and [my college] has an excellent reputation. I knew I wasn't one of the top kids who was going to get a Gates scholarship[9] or something like that, and I knew that getting some aid was just great for me. I didn't know how much I should or shouldn't take out for loans. And actually, I don't know if I would have listened. This was my dream college. It really was."

Carissa acknowledges that she could have taken more initiative in pursuing financial aid. No one in her family had ever gone to college, so it was a foreign concept to them. She knew as a junior in high school that thinking about college was important. "Actually, I knew that college was what I wanted from the moment I got to BAA. But I didn't understand about paying for it. I thought it was something parents paid for, but I had no idea how expensive it was. You know, as a seventeen- or eighteen-year-old, you are so caught up in just getting through high school and all the drama with that, that thinking about money for four years, well that's just huge." With the hindsight of a twentysomething,

Carissa acknowledges she could have done more to prepare herself for life after graduation. "Sometimes the most important thing I thought about in high school was what I was wearing the next day. I know that sounds funny, but it's true!" I had to laugh, remembering Carissa's color-coordinated outfits. She was a theater major, after all, and excelled in costume design. I thought about my own daughter and the kind of support we gave her during the college-application process. She was the youngest and had observed her older brothers writing college essays and banging down the door of the guidance office to get letters of recommendation. When it was her turn to apply for school, she had the luxury of making fashion statements, confident in the fact that her parents were staying on top of deadlines. Carissa knows now that she should have been applying for scholarships the minute senior year started. "But I was doing so much in high school. I was doing my senior project, my dual-enrollment college class, and student government. I had a lot going on. I wasn't thinking scholarships—at least not in October!"

Carissa is not an exception. I've heard from many of my alumni who've been on the receiving end of disparaging comments from financial aid administrators. Navigating the complexities of the college aid system is a shared experience among them. And yet, sadly, responses to their difficulties are similar. Colleagues often say, "How could she have been so unaware?" These comments are often made by people who are not the first in their family to graduate from high school. Of course we want young people to take responsibility for both taking out and then repaying loans. We understand that loans are individually given, but when we approach the entire subject of student debt as solely an individual problem, it prevents us from grappling with larger systemic issues about college access and completion. It's easier to lay blame than to question why we have burdened young people, already burdened by poverty or immigration status, to find their way, largely without support, through the complex system of college aid. Carissa is also not an exception in terms of being locked out of receiving her college credits until she pays back all her loans. We have created unreasonable expectations. Neil Swidey argues in a recent *Boston Globe* piece that students should at least receive the credits they have already paid for.[10] In other words, since Carissa had paid for a year of college, she should be able to claim those credits. Swidey quotes Massachusetts Attorney General Maura Healey, who states, "Students have a right to what they have paid for, including the right to a transcript reflecting their completion of courses. At a time of unprecedented, often crippling student loan debt," colleges should review "their policies to make sure they are balanced and consistent with the school's educational mission." It is within the purview of a college president to stop this unfair practice of denying students access to their own transcripts.

Compare Carissa to my daughter. Both are wonderful young people who should have equally bright futures. But for Carissa money is an obstacle to everything. As a society, we will all suffer if we cannot ensure that students like Carissa can realize her potential. How will we grow as a nation if there is always a population who, because of a lack of resources, will be denied opportunities to pursue their dreams and develop their talents?

In middle- and upper-middle-class families, an invisible safety net typically surrounds young people planning to go on to college. There is usually a family member or friend who will step in and remind a student about the intricacies of student loans and deadlines, or the many requirements for staying registered once enrolled, or issues that can arise with housing. These kinds of conversations are commonplace at many dinner tables and part of numerous e-mail correspondences. However, if you are a lower-income student and you miss one or two e-mails or have a change in your advisor, you may find your dreams derailed. It may be tempting to dismiss the examples above as ineptitude or carelessness on the part of individual students, but why must there be different rules, expectations, and outcomes for low-income versus middle- or upper-income students?

LEILA: PAY ATTENTION TO E-MAIL

Leila had gotten a full scholarship to a competitive local college. Even though she struggled a great deal the first year with fitting in racially and culturally, she knew that she was getting a great education and was determined to put up with any feelings of isolation. After her freshman year, during which she worked nearly thirty hours a week, she and her parents (both undocumented immigrants) pooled enough money together so that Leila could live in the dorm. The chance to experience college life at its fullest was a dream come true for Leila. However, she recently got in touch with me to say that when she went to register for spring classes, she was shocked to find that her account had been frozen. She knew that she had been late with her November payment for housing, but she had gone to the housing office and had worked out a payment plan. "I knew I had cleared up that issue," she said. She went to the student account office to try to figure out what was going on and how what she assumed was a mistake could be rectified. "I was really stressed out. It was midterms and I didn't need to be spending all this time running around to all these offices. I just wanted my hold to be lifted." Leila was horrified to find out that before the college would remove the hold, she had to pay $2,000 immediately. She couldn't figure out what that fee was for. After many more visits to myriad offices, she found out that she was being billed for health insurance. "I was just stunned, since I have MassHealth [the Massachusetts health-insurance program for low-income residents] already and I don't need the college's insurance. I knew I had waived it when I started college." What Leila didn't realize is that she had to renew the waiver every year. She went back and checked her e-mails and saw that, indeed, the college had sent her an e-mail asking if she wanted to waive her insurance. At this point Leila could barely speak. "I'm always on top of my e-mails and I am good at answering them. How I missed this one e-mail, I just don't know. But I did. But the thing is, why didn't I get another e-mail saying that now I would be *charged* for insurance?"

Some may say that the responsibility was on Leila. She should have checked. She should have known. But Leila was making her way through the college system, and all the paperwork, completely on her own. Her parents are not English speakers, and even though Leila had given them access to her student account, they are not computer savvy nor do they understand the various costs that college students incur. There is no support system to see Leila through the intricacies of college life and financing. As she told me, "I think what frustrates me the most is that my college is such a well-known school that it just assumes that every college student has the resources and means to navigate the system. But that's just not true. I didn't." Leila had worked with the director of student success at the college, who had been a terrific advocate, but even that administrator was unable to come up with an acceptable resolution, beyond putting Leila on an additional payment plan. As Leila explained, "I already have a payment plan for room and board. If I had to do this plan, it would put me close to two thousand dollars a month for the next five months. I am sure you know I cannot afford that." Of course Leila considered moving back home, but her family, in order to help her pay for room and board, had moved further out of the city, and the commute to school would have been nearly impossible. She knew her grades would suffer if she were not living on campus. Leila ended up calling me to help her untangle this web. Eventually, the costs were waived and she was given a discounted housing plan. But it took many hours and days of continuous calls and e-mails on the part of an adult advocate (in this case, me) for the issue to be worked out.

Some may continue to insist that if students like Leila want to reap the benefits of college they must assume the responsibilities of a college student, including staying abreast of enrollment requirements. We must recognize, however, how daunting the sometimes-byzantine college system can be to students lacking sufficient support, especially those entering the system at a financial disadvantage.

KEVIN'S STORY

Kevin remembers being encouraged to dream big about college. He knew he was talented. He had excellent grades in both visual arts and academics. "We had heard since we came here [to BAA] as freshmen, even in freshman orientation, that we could all go to college. It was part of the curriculum." Kevin recalls the intensity of senior year with his peers. Classes revolved around writing college essays and preparing portfolios as well as practicing for interviews. "'Where are you applying? Is your portfolio finished?' That's all we talked about. Everyone was going to go somewhere." In this case, the assumption was, there is a college for everyone.

Kevin received a full scholarship to Massachusetts College of Art and Design, a four-year, public arts college, but he desperately wanted what he called the "full college experience" of going away from home and being around a diverse mix of kids. "I'd been doing art so intensely for four years in high school. I just wanted to see what else was out there." So instead of going to MassArt, where he had a full scholarship, he went to another state school: University of Massachusetts Dartmouth, where he would need financial aid. Pell Grants wouldn't cover the cost of in-state tuition with room and board. Qualifying for financial aid wasn't a problem for Kevin, and he understood that he would have to repay some loans when he graduated.

During freshman and sophomore year Kevin had a great advisor who made sure that he did all his financial-aid paperwork on time. But junior year, he was assigned a new advisor in his major. That advisor didn't know Kevin well, and he wasn't as methodical about checking in with Kevin about issues such as aid deadlines. Kevin recalls when his life began to unravel. "I was so busy at the end of sophomore year. I was working for Unity House [for students of color], and I was performing and deejaying all over to earn money for books and everything. I was also working thirty hours a week in the cafeteria. Of course I had a full load of classes too." When he returned in September of his junior year, he discovered he didn't have housing. "Alarm bells should have gone off. I should have realized right away something was wrong. But I just thought it was a housing thing and it would work out. Lots of my friends had had housing issues. So I stayed on a friend's couch for September, waiting for housing to come through. That wasn't so unusual with my friends. But when I went to the housing office to find out when I'd get a room, they just laughed and said I wasn't even enrolled. There was a hold on my account. I was so confused. How could that be? I was like big man on campus. Everyone knew me and loved me. I was involved in everything. Why would I have a hold?" Too late, Kevin realized that he had neglected to apply for financial aid for his junior year.

It was already mid-October and he was too embarrassed to tell his mother that he actually wasn't a student. "She just wouldn't have understood. She had sacrificed her whole life for me to get here." He stayed involved with all his college activities. He kept his on-campus job and even kept going to classes, but slowly things began to catch up with him, and he realized that now he had all this debt and he didn't know what to do. He dropped out of college and worked two jobs trying to pay off some of the loans, but he couldn't make much of a dent in the debt he was accumulating while also paying for rent and food. "It felt like the Great Wall of China. The debt just went higher and higher with the interest. At some point I think I realized that I owed forty-two thousand dollars and there was literally no way I could be paying that off and live." Kevin didn't want to acknowledge that his dreams of a college degree had vanished. He was working forty hours a week cooking in a diner and also making money on the weekends performing and deejaying, but he still couldn't see how he'd ever be able to return to school.

He knows that he should have been responsible for understanding when and how to reapply for financial aid, but he also recognizes the role that his first advisor had played in helping him keep track of the paperwork. "I shouldn't have relied on my advisor, but, you know, if you don't grow up knowing all about financial aid and the deadlines, and you don't have a parent to remind you, it's really important that someone at college can help with that. I'm not the only one who missed deadlines. Sometimes I think colleges should be measured on how many students actually graduate rather than how many enroll. And if a lot drop out, like what happened to me, maybe tuition and loans should be even less. Why isn't the college held responsible at all?"

I'm intrigued by Kevin's last comment. Why, indeed, don't we hold colleges responsible for graduation rates? And how are graduation rates tied to money? There is a direct correlation between the ability to access financial aid and graduation rates. At UMass Dartmouth, graduation rates are under 50 percent. How much of that attrition is due to the fact that money is an obstacle for too many students? I don't think this disappointing graduation rate means that UMass Dartmouth is a bad school. Many of my students who have gone there, whether or not they have graduated, have spoken in positive terms about their classes and the education they received. Even though many students commute, BAA graduates have found that UMass Dartmouth has a strong community of color but offers few programs that adequately help first-generation students, especially with respect to financing. There are no required meetings for these students. There are no regular check-ins. Kevin was lucky to be assigned such an attentive advisor his first few semesters. But luck should not be the reason students graduate or not.

WHY GO TO COLLEGE?

The data on earning gaps between the college-educated and non-college-educated are compelling. The US Bureau of Labor Statistics reports that there is a significant difference in employment and lifetime earnings between those with only a high school education and those with some degree of higher education. The average weekly salary for an individual with only a high school degree is $651, compared with $777 for those with an associate's degree. With a bachelor's degree, the average national weekly salary jumps to $1,108.[11] As a high school headmaster, I pushed college because of the statistical connection to a middle-class life. Doesn't everyone deserve to go to college? Especially *my* students? (A question that will be explored in chapter 4.)

At the same time, the current student-debt crisis has called into question the value of college. Writing in the *Boston Globe Magazine*, Neil Swidey critiqued the "truism about college lifting low-income students out of their circumstances, Horatio Alger style."[12] While we applaud access to higher education, we should be cautious about college degrees that come with staggering amounts of debt. An NPR series has explored the issue of college loans.[13] To cover expenses, many students must work their way through college, but taking a full course load while working up to thirty hours a week can jeopardize grades and thus completion rates. Students who drop out of college are much more likely to default on college loans than those who complete college. The 2016 presidential campaign generated a range of ideas for bringing down the cost of tuition and fees, especially in public colleges and universities. The issue of cost, loans, and debt is more exaggerated at the less well-endowed private colleges. Low-income students at elite colleges such as Harvard and Amherst usually have a free ride and almost no extra expenses, but this is available only to a small minority of the college-going population. Only a few are my students.[14]

The largest percentage of BAA seniors attend in-state colleges, but many strive to get scholarships at private institutions offering superb training in their majors. Some are desperate to get away from home—even if only for a year. They aspire to the same dreams as students all over the United States: college is a stepping-stone to a better future. Yet there is evidence that casts doubt on the widely held consensus that college graduates earn more money than those who did not attend college. Data showing that college graduates' wages are *not* rising proportionally with tuition costs and, further, that many college grads are finding it difficult to find work.[15] Today, close to 9 percent of college grads are out of work. In 2007, 5.5 percent of college graduates under the age of twenty-five were out of work. Are there too many college graduates? Are they in the "wrong" fields? What economic theory can explain these disparities? In 1980, only one in six Americans twenty-five and older were college graduates. As of 2015, about 70 percent of all high school graduates now go on to college, and half of all Americans between the ages of twenty-five and thirty-four have a college degree.

Many argue that a traditional liberal arts college education has value beyond that indicated in a cost-benefit analysis. The purpose of college is both career preparation and personal development. Many educators agree that college provides a unique opportunity for young people to experience rich interpersonal relationships. We embrace the notion that learning to think critically as well as expansively are important attributes for self-development. We stress the importance of learning a second language or taking an array of courses in unfamiliar fields. It is why so many colleges require students to take courses and credits outside their established major. As parents, many want our children to develop a "life of the mind," and we send our children to college precisely so that they can have these broad and deep experiences. BAA, like other schools, wants its students to love learning and build social and economic capital—not just for themselves but for their larger communities.

Maria's story supports that philosophy, but the decision she had to make illuminates that her college dreams were constrained by a lack of access to economic capital. Maria went to a private college out of state. She didn't qualify for much federal aid and only received a small institutional scholarship. Her mother was willing to take out a loan for that first year. "I had a great time there. I was so happy to have the real college experience. The one you always think about—going away from home, living in a dorm, meeting people from all over. I loved it, really, everything about it. I made lots of new friends. You know, I'm such a friendly and open person. I had great classes. I was so excited by each one: Introduction to Anthropology. Psychology. Criminal Justice. I even loved my writing seminar. We had such great discussions in class. I loved that. But after the first year, my family couldn't take out so much in loans anymore. I had to come home. I went to Bunker Hill Community College and got my associate's degree." Now Maria is getting a job in the allied health field. It won't pay a lot, but it has stability. She will start helping her mother pay back her loans from that first year at private school. "I had my fun, but now I just have to work." I wanted to know if she had any regrets about leaving the college that she so enjoyed. Had she felt that she had settled for less? Her response was much more mature than I would have expected. "That's not really the way I can think about things. I have to work. I always knew that. At least I have a job. A lot of people in my family don't. Maybe one day I'll go back to school. Maybe one day I'll study what I really want—psychology and criminal justice. But for now, I'm okay." For Maria, being "okay" meant helping her mother and younger siblings have opportunities too. She was willing to put aside her own dreams in order to support others in her family. Although Maria certainly understands the rules of the game, it is clear to me that had she come from a family with greater financial resources, she would have had the same choices as my own children.

While individuals can certainly benefit from a college degree, society also benefits from young people who have learned to share ideas at high levels as well as to constructively disagree. In a country composed of people from a wide range of backgrounds and experiences, college is an excellent opportunity to learn about people different from oneself. In a recent piece in the *New Yorker*, author John Cassidy acknowledges the important role that a college education has played in shaping the United States.[16] "Promoters of higher education have long emphasized its role in meeting civic needs," Cassidy writes. "The Puritans who established Harvard were concerned about a shortage of clergy; during the Progressive Era, John Dewey insisted that a proper education would make people better citizens, with enlarged moral imaginations." Today we might argue that for the survival of democracy we need educated and engaged citizens. We need citizens who can critically evaluate sources as well as weigh evidence objectively in order to serve successfully on a jury, for example. Now more than ever, we need to understand and put into practice the values on which this country was founded. We cannot diminish the importance of education for nation building. That is the civic imperative.

There is a strong belief in this country that a liberal arts degree is not about job skills or acquisition per se, but rather access to a more dignified and enriched life. A liberal arts degree can provide experiences and knowledge that extend beyond any one individual job. Despite some evidence to the contrary, we still have reason to believe that a college degree can increase social mobility. "A recent study by researchers at the Federal Reserve Bank of San Francisco showed that children who are born into households in the poorest fifth of the income distribution are six times as likely to reach the top fifth if they graduate from college," wrote John Cassidy.[17]

That is certainly what I preached at BAA. I wanted my students—all of them—to have access to college. I knew that few of them would earn admittance into the country's elite colleges, but I believed that even a two-year community college degree would help.

THE HIDDEN COST OF COMMUNITY COLLEGES

It turns out that it matters what kind of college kids go to. The differences between graduation completion rates and later job possibilities for a graduate of Harvard or a graduate of Salem State University (a public school in Massachusetts) are vast. *Crossing the Finish Line: Completing College at America's Public Universities*, by William Bowen, Matthew Chingos, and Michael McPherson, reveals the alarmingly low graduation rates at public colleges and universities. Their research, using data from the National Education Longitudinal Study,[18] demonstrates that socioeconomically disadvantaged students are overrepresented at institutions with low graduation rates and underrepresented at schools with high graduate rates. The authors argue that "attending a more selective institution *increases* students' graduation possibilities."[19] Because the campus environment at flagship universities (as opposed to the various state or community colleges) contributes to an increased proportion of low-socioeconomic-status college graduates, "peer effects . . . and the role of norms or expectations" raise the graduation rates of less advantaged students. The culture of the university pushes everyone toward completing their degree.

The peer environment that supports higher graduation rates at more selective institutions does not extend to community colleges. Yet, in my desire to see my students attend college, I encouraged students to go to these much more affordable schools, even if they had to take developmental classes. But the study cited above raises concerns about the connection between money and the actual experience of students at community colleges. It really matters if a student in a community college is placed in developmental or college-credit-bearing classes. Financial aid does not cover the tuition for developmental classes; students must pay out of pocket. Community colleges have a very open admissions policy. However, all students must take a test, called the Accuplacer, to see whether they have the requisite skills to enter credit-bearing courses. This creates a whole new layer of inequity. Take the following example, which demonstrates how this system continues to disadvantage already disadvantaged students.

Marcel had done very well at BAA. He had an Individualized Education Program to support his learning disability and was a talented visual artist. When he visited MassArt, the admissions director explained that she thought it would be beneficial for Marcel to go for two years to Bunker Hill Community College (BHCC), which has an articulation agreement with MassArt to ensure the seamless transition of credits from one campus to another. Other BAA students had followed this path. After taking courses at BHCC, they had transferred to MassArt or UMass Boston with a year's worth of credits—and at a substantial cost savings. Marcel started at BHCC, but because of his score on the Accuplacer test, he was placed in developmental classes. Accuplacer tests are developed by the College Board to assess reading, writing, math, and computer skills. Students are placed in either developmental or general education classes based on their scores. Marcel was determined to finish his classes and move on. He took out a loan to cover the cost, but after two years, he still had not been able to get the requisite score on the Accuplacer test. Many colleges, including public ones such as Salem State, have stopped using the SAT as part of the admissions system, but public *community* colleges have insisted on keeping the Accuplacer test. The very students who do poorly on standardized tests, like Marcel, are kept in a kind of educational gulag. After two years of developmental courses, which he passed, Marcel gave up and left BHCC with a hefty debt and nothing to show for it. It is likely that he would have done fine in other BHCC courses. He was motivated to do the work, but continued to be a lousy test taker. The Accuplacer test results essentially overruled the grades he received in his classes.

When, in 2015, I spoke with Carlos Santiago, Massachusetts's higher education commissioner, we discussed the dismal statistics of students in developmental or remedial classes. In 2010, there were twelve thousand students in community colleges in need of remediation in math. Two years later, only two thousand of those students had completed a regular-education math class.[20] The remaining students had fallen off the grid. To Santiago, this was unacceptable. He initiated a pilot program to move away from Accuplacer and use GPA for placement. The results were very positive over a short period of time, and more students succeeded at higher rates than those who had used Accuplacer for placement. Pam Eddinger, president of Bunker Hill Community College, also acknowledges the potentially detrimental effects of the Accuplacer test. She argues, as does Commissioner Santiago, that GPA, transcripts, recommendations, and even student choice must account for course placement. Eddinger feels strongly that students, because of aspirations and motivation, could go right into the college-level class—as long as they understand what they are getting into—while taking a complementary class that provides additional support. She posits that with tutoring and coaching and motivation, students often exceed expectations.[21] This is very similar to the model used with special education students in pre-K–12 grades in which the student will often have a "learning center" class that is slower paced, and smaller, to review concepts and get extra help at the same time that they are enrolled in the regular academic class. Eddinger suggests diagnostic tests should be used so that students understand what this test says about their skills, but that one test result should not be a barrier for accessing more rigorous coursework. I wish this kind of system had been in place for Marcel.

We know that a student's score on one test is not an indicator of intelligence, or even skills. It is only an indicator of the skills and knowledge for that one test. Moreover, there is evidence that Accuplacer doesn't accurately predict student success. As Judith Scott-Clayton, an assistant professor in economics and education at Columbia University, says, "It's hard to predict who is going to do well in college-level courses on the basis of these one-off, relatively short exams."[22]

Marcel had never done well on tests. But he had mastered all of BAA's requirements, such as the twenty-page humanities paper and senior visual arts exhibition. He knows how to access help and he understands how to work hard. Sadly, his fate is now sealed and a degree in visual arts is not in his future.

We have had many other students with academic records similar to Marcel's go to private two-year (and four-year) colleges and graduate in much higher numbers. In fact, Marcel's classmate Freddie, a dancer, who had similar academic issues, got into Dean College, a private college with an excellent track record of supporting students with learning disabilities. Dean also has a strong dance department. Private colleges do not use the Accuplacer. Freddie graduated with a strong record and is now running a video business in California where his clients are mostly artists. Had he been subjected to the Accuplacer test, he may have never graduated. In lieu of placement tests such as Accuplacer, some open-access colleges have started using a variety of assessments. For instance, Long Beach City College began using high school grades as a measurement, and as a result, more students have passed college-level courses.[23] More public community colleges should follow the model of Long Beach City College and revisit their rigid adherence to the Accuplacer, which relegates too many students to developmental classes. In Massachusetts, there are cases of students who have passed AP Calculus and failed Accuplacer.[24]

In the meantime, I suggest that we change financial aid policies to cover developmental courses for a year. We cannot condone a system that doubly burdens our most vulnerable students. Our goal should be to ensure that more students can take more college courses, not fewer. We cannot continue to limit access by one test, especially if that test ends up creating an undue financial burden on our students. Or what if we make community college tuition-free, including developmental classes? More importantly, perhaps a new policy could be introduced that after a year of developmental classes, a student can petition to take a general education class. We must not forget that success begets more success and repeated failure only creates fewer incentives for students to take risks and prove what they know.

As a school leader, I always said that the outcomes for our most vulnerable students determined our success. It's relatively easy to educate those who arrive with solid skills and support from home. But the real measure of our efforts should be with those students that we truly teach, those students who are not already inoculated against school failure, if you will. The same is true in the larger society. Our worth as a nation cannot be determined just by the achievement of our most gifted students. We must keep a laser focus on those who start way behind the eight ball.

COMPETENCY-BASED COLLEGE: A TWO-TIERED ALTERNATIVE?

There have been other responses to address the impact of money as an obstacle for college completion. For example, Southern New Hampshire University confronts the question of "was college a waste of time and money?" by offering an online, competency-based option for a degree through College for America. Instead of offering the full college experience, the program offers competency-based classes that are focused on finishing a degree and obtaining a good job. College for America programs partner with employers who want to further develop their workforce. The front page of its website reads: "College for America is an accredited, nonprofit college dedicated to making a college degree achievable for every working adult: flexibly scheduled, uniquely applicable, competency-based for just $3,000 a year (or less)."[25] Credit hours, professors, and traditional classes have been replaced by a series of competencies that students must complete satisfactorily, at their own pace.

Match Education, a K–12 charter organization, is now expanding into higher education and has partnered with College for America. Match Beyond is a not-for-profit organization whose mission is "to enable low-income young adults in Boston to achieve their college degrees and attain middle class employment" through online courses and weekly meetings with coaches.[26] Match Beyond has paired with College for America to create another avenue for young people, between the ages of eighteen and thirty-five, who have dropped out and may have debt but still want a college degree. This relatively new initiative is in response to the fact that many graduates of urban high schools don't graduate from college. Some of the early designers of this partnership were dismayed because, even after strong high school preparation for college, Match alumni were not finishing college at the rate their teachers had hoped. The reasons given resonate with what my BAA alumni told me: cost and debt, inadequate preparation or fit, and the reality that life—pregnancy, illness, family obligations, work—can get in the way of schooling. Match, in collaboration with College for America and Southern New Hampshire University, is trying to get the cost of college down to its core: a series of online projects and assignments that add up to a degree. According to Match CEO Stig Leschley, so much of the cost of college is bound up in the campus experience—dorm living, dining halls with abundant choices of meals, sports teams and extravagant athletic facilities for students, and the leafy green grounds. Leschley and other leaders in a competency-based approach to college argue that the only way to get down the cost for students is to radically pare down all the accoutrements of college and provide the bare essentials—the taking and passing of "rigorous, job-based" courses. Although many critique the rigor of competency-based college courses, College for America is considered one of the strongest providers. Nevertheless, the federal government has been slow to jump into the competency-based market and only awards Title IV grants for financial aid to a limited number of colleges and universities. This is because of the limited evidence that such courses are, in fact, high quality. Others argue that a competency-based degree is fine for entry into a working-class job but few doctors, lawyers, teachers, or others in the professional class would choose such a degree. For many, college is more than an accumulation of online experiences; it is the "gestalt" of being in an intellectual environment. It *is* also the experience of living in a dorm, experiencing new food, being able to work out in a gym at 1 a.m., having myriad different professors and friends, and exploring the life of the mind in face-to-face discussions. Match Beyond advocates concede that the "college experience" works for many but note that there are more than thirty thousand young people in Boston alone who either never went to college or dropped out, and who, in order to access middle-class employment, need, and deserve, a college degree. College for America's online platform is a different way to get that degree, and Match Beyond is developing programming to support students to succeed in that environment.

When I asked Match leaders why they wouldn't just provide the same kind of life coaching and supports to students at community colleges that students at four-year institutions receive, they noted the low success rates at community colleges. They also claimed that they had been unable to develop the kind of partnerships with community colleges that College for America offered. Further, community college courses are time-based as opposed to competency-based, and for Match's clientele the flexibility is critical. Furthermore, College of America pays Match $2,500 per student to provide the surround-care support that these students need. While this doesn't cover Match's total costs (and they provide tutoring, one-on-one coaching, and a place to study in downtown Boston), it is certainly more than a community college could ever conceive of paying. Community colleges in Massachusetts receive approximately $4,000 per student. Students in vocational programs, just to give a comparison, receive $17,000 per person. It seems that Match, Inc., has decided that more students with college degrees, no matter how the degrees are achieved, is better than fewer students with college degrees, especially if those students are racking up high debt.

I am left wondering about the creation of a two-tiered system: one with all the bells and whistles of college as we have come to know it, and the other, a drastically pared-down version that is just about getting the degree. I also wonder how a College for America degree is valued in the open market. The programs that the college runs with companies like Panera Bread or other large corporations are specifically about skill building for that industry, but what does a general bachelor's degree from College for America signify? How will a graduate school view the diploma if a student wants to continue with advanced studies? The research on competency-based higher education is still in its developmental stage, and I worry that the current experimentation may condemn young people to low-wage jobs. Nonetheless, College for America's commitment to radically lower the cost of higher education is a commendable first step.

While I have been considering this dual system and questioning its possibilities, for-profit colleges have also entered the market, for the most part preying on student dissatisfaction with access to college. But, they are also not cheap. Tuition is five to six times higher than community colleges and twice that of state universities. Twenty to twenty-five percent of for-profit colleges' budgets are dedicated to sales and marketing. Their presence in poor communities is especially ubiquitous. Recruiters have been criticized for exploiting what are often called "student pain points," such as, "Do you really want to work at McDonald's the rest of your life?" or, "Don't you want to do better than your parents?"

FOR-PROFIT COLLEGES

The experience of our few graduates that find their way to these for-profit schools has been devastating. One student, Jay, ended up at a for-profit college in New Hampshire to pursue a career in music recording. In high school, Jay was surrounded by other students who were applying for college and financial aid. However, his grades and academic preparation were not as strong as his peers', and so when the time came to apply for college, he had fewer choices. His family situation had deteriorated, and he wanted to get away from the negative influences of his old neighborhood, which threatened to derail everything he had worked for during high school. Staying in Boston and attending community college became less of an option. A teacher drove him to visit a for-profit school, and both were impressed by the school's stunning facilities. Jay's mom and pastor agreed that it was best for Jay to get out of the city, so the decision was made to take out a loan.

The school had promoted its ties to the recording industry and record of job placement for students earning a two-year associate's degree. However, when Jay, after a year in the college and in a great deal of debt, wanted to transfer his credits to a different music college, he was told that the credits wouldn't be recognized. Jay was shattered. He was without credits that counted and had huge loans and no promise of a job to help him pay back his loans. Jay's experience reflects that of students from other for-profit institutions.

Unlike many other victims of for-profit false advertising, Jay was fortunate to have always been involved with the church. His pastor was willing to pay for him to go to Bible school to be a minister. When I talked to Jay recently, he was calmer about his situation. "Maybe that year was a way to bring me closer to God," he said. He added that he's feeling more confident about his future and having a church of his own one day. He knows he will be paying the loans back for a long time, but at least he is studying what matters to his heart and soul. "I don't know, perhaps I'll give a sermon one day on the evils of those kind of schools. They sure fooled me." Jay is more generous in his assessment than others I've met.

Although only 13 percent of students nationally attend a for-profit college, they account for one-third of all student loans and debt.[27] And though for-profit colleges continue to boast of high graduation and job-acquisition rates, many of these claims have come under increased scrutiny and criticism for being way overblown. One national chain of for-profit colleges, ITT Technical Institute, has revealed grim statistics. Out of a class of 175 students, at one of their campuses, 75 percent did not graduate and only 13 percent found work in their field![28] After a federal investigation on how recruiters prey on veterans, Corinthian Colleges also began to either sell or close many of their campuses. Once the second largest for-profit chain in the country, Corinthian ultimately went bankrupt (in 2015), but not before it was found to have lied about job placements over one thousand times.[29] In September 2016, ITT also closed, leaving tens of thousands of students in debt and without degrees.[30]

Not enough critical attention has been given to the tactics and outcomes of colleges in the for-profit sector. These schools have made promises that they cannot keep. And yet, the federal government subsidizes more than 90 percent of the steep tuition at for-profit colleges. According to a study by the economists Adam Looney and Constantine Yannelis, students at for-profit schools are "roughly three times as likely to default as students at traditional colleges. And the ones who don't default often use deferments to stay afloat."[31] Since the schools themselves were not lending money, but rather utilizing the taxpayer-funded financial aid system, the for-profit sector had little incentive to worry about whether loans would be paid back. While this tactic, or gaming of the system, may not directly be against the law, should our federal dollars be invested in supporting institutions that take advantage of our most vulnerable youth and our veterans? Hopefully, as a result of recent investigations, the government will begin to make it more difficult for colleges in the for-profit sector to easily prey on students' desire for a quality higher education.

Jay's situation raises a host of other questions about how high schools prepare students for college. It's easy to play Monday-morning quarterback and say, "We should have never let Jay go off to *that* college." However, there are often limited options for a young person for whom money is an extraordinary obstacle. To conclude that Jay's mistake was being poor and needing to get out of the city is patently unfair. We must change the way we think about the Jays in our high schools. We must be vigilant about ensuring that they have better choices, and we need the government to begin cracking down on the practices at for-profit colleges. Most of all, we need to carefully consider how we make college affordable and accessible for all.

LOOKING TOWARD THE FUTURE

Learning about how many of my alumni like Raul have left college with huge loans and debts, perhaps more cynical readers will say: "They should have never gone to college in the first place." Or worse, "They went to third-tier schools that did not have the resources to support them." There may be truth in those statements. But Raul is not an exception or a mistake. He represents many young people in this country who are neither supported by family income nor sufficiently by college or federal loans. In fact, while debt at private universities and colleges has only increased by 3 percent a year since 2006, debt at public colleges has increased by 20 percent a year.[32] What can shift in our policies so that many students, like my alumni, do not remain on the fringes of society, in low-wage jobs, recalling high school as the time that they were the most empowered or engaged?

As Kevin said to me, "The thing about UMass–Dartmouth is that a lot of us are first-generation college-going kids. We don't have parents at home that know about the college or how to pay for it, or any of that. But we are sort of like the American dream. We are like what this country is made from. And if we don't make it, I can't help but wonder if the whole country will make it." Said differently, if as a society we can't figure out how to support the young people who attend UMass Dartmouth, for example, where does that leave huge swaths of the population? And what does that say about our democracy? Large numbers of students dropping out or owing a huge amount of loan debt cannot be good for our overall economic stability. We aspire to an educated population who can contribute to an ever-thriving economy. Furthermore, if there are not rigorous investigations and conversations across our college and universities about retention and graduation rates, broken down by racial and socioeconomic groups, how will we ever address the growing disparities in achievement in this country? Not until higher education is accessible to all, will all constituents have an equal voice in our democracy. This cannot just be a K–12 conversation. Institutions of higher education have a responsibility to graduate the students they accept.

There are vastly different perceptions and assumptions about debt in this country. As Joseph Stiglitz says, "Student debt has become an integral part of the story of American inequality. Robust higher education, with healthy public support, was once the linchpin in a system that promised opportunity for dedicated students of any means. We now have a pay-to-play, winner-take-all game where the wealthiest are assured a spot, and the rest are compelled to take a gamble on huge debts, with no guarantee of a payoff."[33] Perhaps the confusion harkens back to an earlier point: Who is advantaged by the assumption that money isn't an obstacle to a college degree? I don't want to assume that there is a full-blown conspiracy in this country against low-income students, but the ingrained belief in a meritocracy works against low-income, first generation students, and particularly students of color. The idea that you may not "look poor," as Carissa found out, can make the byzantine system of financial aid even more obtuse and difficult to navigate. There is no lobby for low-income students to have better access to college. Although the 2016 presidential campaigns had suggestions of free community colleges, which President Barack Obama had also called for, that is only part of the issue. And now, with a Trump administration, it is doubtful we will see any reprieve. In fact, it would not be surprising if for-profit colleges will return in full, unregulated force and continue to prey on poor people.[34]

My students desperately want to believe what we have taught them: They can go to college. Money isn't everything. They will get scholarships. They can even take out loans. Raul, Kevin, Leila, and so many others realize too late that money, in fact, is everything. They also realize that making one small mistake means the difference between securing a future that they dreamed of in high school and a future that may not be better than their parents'. As we will continue to discuss in future chapters, money, white privilege, and the ethos of meritocracy have created extraordinary barriers for too many. We have created a two-tiered system that seems to have no end in sight.

Again, relative privilege ensures this will not happen with my own children. I have been able to help them with college and even graduate school. My son, a medical school student, will be able to make a choice about whether he wants to become a primary care physician and he will not have to enter a more lucrative specialty field just to pay back loans. This kind of freedom shouldn't be available only to the affluent.

I don't have easy solutions for the national trends. But here are some of the ways in which high schools can tackle the problems and ensure that money is less of an obstacle for many students.

1. *Weeklong college-prep intensive for seniors.* BAA, for example, has introduced support for college much earlier in the year. The school now has an August institute for rising seniors to help them with college essay and application writing, narrowing down decisions about which colleges to apply for, as well as information about scholarships and loans. BAA alums and college students from places like Emerson College volunteer to help staff this intensive weeklong experience. It's a step in the right direction. But it is not sufficient. It is staffed by volunteers and the school must fund-raise to pay teachers to return earlier in the year. It is difficult to maintain this level of intense one-on-one support during the year. There are many not-for-profits that also are dedicated to college advising. Might they all come together to offer similar August Institutes for more rising seniors? There are approximately thirty-nine hundred seniors in Boston Public Schools annually, and approximately twenty or more nonprofits providing some

kind of college counseling. Picture the impact on our young people if everyone pooled their resources!

2. *Support for increased numbers of guidance counselors in schools.* Schools are not properly funded to increase the number of guidance counselors. For most high schools the ratio is one counselor for three hundred students. In addition, high schools in America are now excessively burdened by testing and curricular demands and this is where guidance counselors are forced to spend their time as opposed to actual college and career advising. There is little room in the school day or the schedule to attend to the very issues that will make or break a young person's future in college. The introduction of the College Advising Corps, a new nonprofit, has brought recent college graduates into urban schools to support the application process for low-income and first-generation students. Over time, this program could grow and positively impact more students. But we need to decide, as a nation, if we want to parcel out college advising to the nonprofit sector or if we believe that trained and certified guidance counselors belong in our schools in larger numbers. I would suggest a merging of the two: increase funding and increase partnerships.

3. *Hiring of retention specialists.* BAA has also recently received funding from an individual donor to hire a retention specialist to track students particularly during the summer, before they go to college, and through their first year in college, particularly the first semester. Much of the research suggests that if students can make it through that first year, there is a higher correlation to successful college completion. The retention specialist is analyzing data from both 2008 and 2015 BAA graduates to see if there are any specific trends that might help the high school better support alumni and the entire college process. An annual pre-Thanksgiving breakfast has been established which gives students an opportunity to return to BAA, and share their stories, both successes and challenges. The hope is that then BAA can further tailor support to these students. I believe this intervention will greatly assist with graduation completion, but it should be important enough that this is funded for *every* high school in

Boston and in the country, and not just those that are fortunate enough to have wealthy donors.

4. *Financial aid counseling.* BAA has a required financial aid evening early in the fall for seniors. Students are required to bring a parent or older sibling or relative. Ms. Hairston invites financial aid officers from local colleges as well as other experts on financial aid. The intention of the evening is to help everyone understand the complexities of applying for, and then sustaining financial aid. During that evening, Ms. Hairston also makes individual appointments with parents and caregivers so that they can privately review their individual circumstances with her at a later date. As part of this meeting, students are told that in order to graduate they must fill out the financial aid forms. If they do not wish to, parents must at least return the forms saying, "Not interested." We want to ensure that we are not missing anyone in this process. Of course, we have never actually held back a student's diploma if they didn't fill out the form, but it has been an important way to find out who isn't documented or who has no idea what the form means and, therefore, requires more assistance. All high schools can make these evening or weekend sessions required for families. Making FAFSA and the rigors of financial aid understandable to high school students is an imperative. Again, working with local non-profits that regularly do this work could also assist over-burdened high school counselors.

5. *In addition, there needs to be a concerted effort at the high school level to better teach students about debt.* For a few years at BAA, we tried to run a math course related to the stock market, the meaning of credit cards, and debt. These are life skills that need to find their way into the high school curriculum. It is interesting to note that before high-stakes testing overtook curriculum, there were more opportunities at the middle and high school level for courses in "real-life math."

My list of what high schools can do to ensure that money does not continue to be such an obstacle is long, but additional resources are also required. Furthermore, as I've listened to my students, I have become convinced that higher education institutions also have a responsibility to find solutions to alleviate financial constraints for low-income students, first-generation students, and students of color.

1. *Release of transcripts.* All college leaders could agree to release transcripts for courses that students had already paid for. In this way, students would be able to hold on to some of the credits they had earned and not forfeit everything.

2. *Success Offices.* Colleges could commit to robust Success Offices with clear and continuous communication to students. The goal of these offices would be to ensure college completion of enrolled students. Imagine if during the regular orientation students had the chance to work with trained personnel about financial aid deadlines, what you can choose to waive (like health insurance) and myriad other issues that crop up constantly for which many students are unprepared. Imagine if these offices were staffed with students like Leila who understood the invisible web that can trap low-income students too easily.

3. *Additional orientation sessions for first-generation students.* As Leila wisely says, "The Success Office can only do so much. People in the financial aid office, student accounts, health, all those places where we have to interact, also need to know that their job is to help us and not prevent us from graduating." These offices need to hold regular and required meetings for their students.

4. *Professional development on supporting low-income population.* Colleges could collaborate on professional development focused on working with first-gen students for all employees who work in student accounts, financial aid, and other areas. In addition to having good accounting skills, perhaps these employees could benefit from broad training in how to support low-income students in their college going years, including sensitivity training around poverty. As I have said, Carissa's painful experience was described in different versions by many students.

5. *Rethinking accountability for success in rating colleges.* All colleges and universities should be required to publish data that reports graduation rates by "sub-groups." ("Sub-groups" is the term used

by the state to define non-white students, special education students, or students in poverty.) All pre-K–12 public schools' test scores are reported annually in the newspaper and on the Department of Education website by "sub-groups." Why is it that higher education institutions are not obligated to play by the same rules? A professor friend of mine at a four-year "second tier" private college tells me her president doesn't want to release the scores of graduation rates for African American students because they are so abysmal. This lack of transparency renders the crisis difficult to analyze and address.

6. *Debt forgiveness.* Higher education institutions could lobby the federal government so that loan forgiveness programs are widely adopted. This continues to be one of the most serious ways in which low-income young people are trapped.

7. *Rethinking the role of Accuplacer tests in community colleges.* It is clear to me that these tests are serving a harmful role in the advancement of young people. I would like to see community colleges eliminate them and use GPA, recommendations, and transcripts for placement. In so doing, students can take "co-requisite" work alongside their college-level classes.

8. *More investment in community colleges.* As I have noted, per-pupil expenditures in Massachusetts are abysmal. It is difficult to provide the necessary supports to the myriad students who attend community college. I would, ideally, like to see community colleges offering more online, self-paced courses similar to College for America but with more extensive supports for students than community colleges now offer. I would also like to see financial aid cover development courses.

9. *Competency-based college degrees.* I have discussed the program that College for America is working on with Match, Inc. I think these programs need more analysis on outcomes for participants; otherwise, I fear that we are developing a two-tiered system. Nevertheless, I'm intrigued by a pilot program that allows careful analysis of how students do in a non-time-based or credit-based system as compared to a more traditional one. For some students I believe the results will be strong.

Finally, could we imagine a more holistic conversation between higher education leaders, high school principals, guidance counselors, nonprofit leaders and funders—both private and governmental—about the kind of supports necessary to ensure that money is not an obstacle for success in college? Students across the country are engaging in protests about the tiny numbers of students of color attending many of our private and more elite colleges. These Black Lives Matter protests are laudable. They harken back to the student movement of the 1960s. But I fear that the students are missing the point by just demanding higher percentages. Once students are accepted, colleges must be accountable for *graduating* those students. The real question is how all institutions of higher education can ensure that the Kevins and Carissas of this country, and even the Rauls, who made such a damaging mistake, are afforded access to finishing college and earning a degree. If we believe that college access for poor and working-class youth and adults is an important vehicle for democracy to continue to regenerate itself, the entire nation must commit to changing our policies so that money does not continue to be an obstacle.

CHAPTER TWO

"Race Doesn't Matter"

In 2009, the entire student body of BAA gathered in a local college auditorium to watch the inauguration of Barack Obama. The young people—black and white, Latino and Asian—were elated. Teachers held their breath. Surely we had students whose families were avowedly and proudly Republican and had not voted for Obama. We certainly had faculty who had voted for Hillary Clinton in the primaries and a few who had voted for John McCain in the general election. Yet no one could deny the power of the moment. Many of us wondered if inaugurating the first black president in the country's history meant that we were entering a new, postracial era. Articles in the popular media hailed a new age for the United States. Obama's election occurred years before Ferguson. Students, particularly young students of color, were easily swept up in the joy of the historic moment. Was it possible that we were finally putting our racial divisions behind us and that the United States could truly be a meritocracy?

Kendra was a senior in high school at the time. Watching Obama's inauguration, she cried. She was so proud and also frustrated that she hadn't yet been eligible to vote. Many of her friends had voted for Obama, though, and all deeply believed that they were living in a time of great change and hopefulness. Kendra is one of eight students whose stories I will share in this chapter. All but two are students of color. Their experiences and insights teach us much about improving education on several levels—college, high school, and professional development for teachers. Perhaps racism is a less quantifiable obstacle than money, but it affects the quality of life for "minority" students on campus, and can even affect their ability to stay in school. Data on persistence (returning to college after the first year) and attainment (graduating from a four-year program within six years) continues to show great disparities between white students and students of color, particularly black and Hispanic. A 2012 report compiled by the National Council of Educational Statistics found that white students' persistence rates were ten points higher than black or Latino students'.[1] And, as we will discover in this chapter, white students also acknowledge the deleterious effects of racism on their education.

At BAA, Kendra didn't give race much notice. White students were in the minority at about 14 percent. Kendra's friends, whether black or white, mostly talked about their assignments and their artwork. Her advisor and guidance counselor urged Kendra to apply to a small New England college known for its strong art department and ability to support students throughout all four years. Initially, Kendra was dubious. She was a city girl and the idea of going north where there was even more snow made her nervous. Besides, she asked, "Are there any black people up there?"

Her advisor, Ms. Bailor, also a woman of color, laughed and told her that she too had gone to a college with very few black people. "At first it was really weird, but then I kind of liked it. I knew that I wanted to go into a science field and that I would need to know how to work with lots of different people so I thought, why not start now!" Ms. Bailor, who worked in industry before teaching, talked to Kendra about how college taught her how different kinds of cultures or races had different kinds of humor. "I remember that I never got white people's jokes my first few years. And they never really understood much about the things we laughed about. But one day, with my roommate, we had this great talk about that. By the end of the evening, we were both rolling on the floor laughing so hard. That brought us really close." Beyond the experience of appreciating a new kind of humor, Ms. Bailor deeply believed that "integrating" a college was important for her and her peers. She wanted the same for her BAA students. Over the years, we have sent a smattering of students to historically black colleges, most notably Spell-man. While students are often interested in these colleges, the scholar-ships are often limited.

After listening to Ms. Bailor and talking with her mother, Kendra ap-plied to the college with her best friend, Denise, and both were accepted. They received institutional aid as well as generous federal financial aid packages. "We both knew that it would be really different going to col-lege far away, but we had each other and we thought it would be really cool having such a different experience. And we were excited about the art facilities that the college had. We didn't even think that going to col-lege would force us to think so much about race, and money." Kendra's mom also assured her that since the college had given her a scholarship they must have really wanted her to go there.

When neither Kendra's nor Denise's parents could drive them to campus, one of the teachers volunteered. The car ride was a bit tense. The girls kept making fun of all the cows they saw after they turned off the interstate highway. Ms. Kennedy, the teacher, reminded Kendra and Denise that many of the students on campus would come from rural backgrounds and be unfamiliar with city life. She explained that one of the best parts of college is getting to know people from very different places. "Yeah, we can teach them about city life and they can teach us about country life." Both girls giggled to release the nervousness they felt as their destination came into view.

The first few months were really hard for both Kendra and Denise. There were only ten African American students on campus. White class-mates told Kendra they had never sat next to a black person before. "They didn't say it to be mean. But I had never heard that before. I kept think-ing: What do they really mean?" In the evenings, Kendra and Denise would exchange stories about the weird looks or comments that they received on a daily basis. They were learning the term "microaggression" very fast and finding some comfort in knowing they had each other.

Despite feeling alienated, Kendra focused on her studies and her art. She liked her professors and she even liked her classmates, although she felt that so many of their comments and questions were ignorant. She kept thinking, "When is this going to be like the way movies and TV describe college? Meeting and making lots of new friends." Denise was having a really rough time. She didn't get along with her roommate and she found herself subjected to racial microaggressions on a daily basis. "I hate that my writing professor keeps looking to me to answer for all black people whenever the articles have to do with race. What do I know about all black people? I barely know about my own self!" she said, laughing, but she wasn't amused, and she was desperate for Kendra to commiserate with her.

One day the girls were in Denise's room while Denise talked to her mother. "I know, I know, Ma." Denise was practically yelling. "But I get so mad all the time at the stupid things they ask me about how I grew up and what it's like around my way. They all think everyone in my building is always getting shot at or a drug addict!" Denise let out a groan. She nodded her head and seemed to listen to some advice her mom was giving her. "Yeah, all right, I will. Yeah, she's right here. Bye, Ma." Kendra looked at her friend quizzically. "She told me to act more like you, and not get so upset at everything." Kendra let out a laugh and said, "Except it's true that half your building is filled with drug addicts!" Both girls fell on the bed laughing. "Yeah," Denise said, "can you imagine if I invited some of these girls to my house? What would they think, then?" Kendra answered, "Then they'd know you're a crazy b——, just like I know! But stop letting them get to you. Just try and focus on the good things like the amazing studios and stuff." Denise agreed.

Kendra began to get busier with her classes and didn't have as much time to commiserate with Denise. But when her friend began to miss classes and stopped responding to texts and phone calls, Kendra didn't know what to do. Worried that Denise was depressed, Kendra repeatedly went to Denise's room and tried to talk to her, but nothing seemed to help. After Thanksgiving, Denise didn't return. "It was just too hard for her. And her mom didn't really care. Not enough. I mean her mom tried to help with the phone calls and all, but . . ." Kendra's voice trailed off. "You know for both of us college was such a new thing and being in the minority was really different for us. I know it's terrible to say, but I think Denise's mom wanted her to come home, to help with the younger kids. My mom would have killed me if I had dropped out. I wanted to, so many times. She even told me that if I even thought of doing what Denise had done I could *never* come home. That kinda scared me."

Kendra made it through the next two years. She did very well in her art discipline and her college offered her the chance to spend her junior year in Arizona. "It was an amazing opportunity. I knew so many of my friends were going away for their junior year. They called it 'junior year abroad.'" At first she thought it was some special class that everyone took, but as her friends began to talk about going to France or Japan or Mexico, Kendra realized what "abroad" actually meant. She asked her roommate how you find out about those kinds of programs and her roommate took her to the Study Abroad Office. "I hadn't even known that it existed, but everyone else seemed to know. I was so embarrassed when I found out that my scholarship didn't cover study abroad." But it turned out that the college did have a program at Arizona State University (ASU). "I was so excited when I heard that. To me, that was like going abroad. Arizona was as far away for me as France. So I went."

She describes how different it was to go to ASU, a college where she was not one of ten people of color. "I felt liberated. I felt safe. I felt almost like I was back at BAA." Kendra got very involved in ethnic studies and political movements. She had friends from around the world and from every different ethnic and racial group. The riots and protests in Ferguson happened when she was in Arizona and she was moved by the various ways student organizations mobilized and protested. "I was involved in so many discussions with so many different people—Mexican American, Hawaiian, African American—and with so much more diversity on the faculty." She thought about transferring to ASU and doing her senior year there, but she realized that her mother and grandmother would never be able to afford to come to graduation and seeing her graduate was incredibly important to them, and to Kendra. She was also worried about her little sister. "I wanted to be closer to her too."

Although she was sad, she returned to her homogenous New England college, and, armed with newly minted political skills, she started to organize a Black Student Union. She wanted to find a way to question why there were so few faculty of color and why there was no concentration in ethnic or African American studies. She reminded the administration about the positive impact that having had a resident artist from another country and culture—not to mention a Black South African who had lived through apartheid—had brought the year before.

Particularly students of color had appreciated learning from someone who had experienced such intense oppression. She was stunned by the reaction of the college administration to her suggestions. "They actually asked: 'Why do you need to call it a Black Student Union?' I knew enough not to laugh aloud. They were serious. That doesn't sound inclusive to me. They actually said that too."

Although there were only eleven African American students on campus, they formed the first ever Black Student Union. On campus, the group organized non-violent protests against the Ferguson decision. "We did prayers for peace and got lots of other students involved, but the administration was so paranoid. They were sure we were going to be violent. Now, why would they think that?" Kendra answered her own question. "In their minds, just seeing all the black students together meant that something crazy was going to happen." Kendra was hurt, insulted, and angry, but she wasn't going to let the administration know it. "You know, I'd been an RA all sophomore year and now again as a senior, so I was trusted to help run a dorm but not to start an important organization that would give students a chance to voice their disgust and anger at what was going on in the country!"

Nevertheless, Kendra persevered and was very active in the Black Student Union her entire senior year. When I asked Kendra to talk about her four years in college and what she was most grateful for, her answer surprised me. "I've learned so much about different people," she said. "I think back on my first year and how I didn't really want to get to know all those girls from the country that had never met a black person before, but now they know me and I think their attitudes have changed. I want to go into marketing and advertising, and so I'm glad I know about different people. I'm not so judgmental. And the best thing: the Black Student Union is really strong. The black students who were freshmen and sophomores when I was a senior really have made it their own. Maybe there will even be an Africana studies major there one day!"

Denise is proud that Kendra finished. "I wish I could have been strong enough. I really do. But I got too depressed." She acknowledges that her mom wasn't as committed to her staying as Kendra's was. "You know if you complain to your mom, and she says, "Well okay, come home," then that's what you do. I wish I hadn't, but I didn't have anyone pushing me, and it was just too lonely up there for me." Denise conceals her disappointment a little by saying, "Well, my mom really needed me at home too. I was the only one that my little sister listened to." She says she'll go back to school again when her sister straightens out. "And I'll make sure when she goes to college she understands what microaggression means and how to deal with [it]. That was all so new to me."

Ms. Bailor and I have discussed why some students, like Kendra, make it and others, like Denise, drop out. There are no easy answers. For some students, the racial microaggressions are just too difficult to take. For others, they know that this is part of what going to college is all about. I keep wondering how we could have prepared Denise better.

MELISSA'S STORY: THE IMPORTANCE OF A GROUP

For observers outside situations like Kendra's or Denise's, comfortable conclusions could be "they should have known," or "they weren't ready," or "they were too sensitive," or "not everything is about race." Rather than finding individual fault with students like Denise, I find value in pointing out ways in which they are doubly burdened. The majority of our colleges are overwhelmingly white, and the accepted behaviors, attitudes, and ways of maneuvering a new campus and situation are often second nature to white students. Wanting to believe that race doesn't matter, or isn't an obstacle to success in college, is inviting a shortsighted view that denies an important reality. More deliberate work at the high school level to prepare our students for college in a racially biased world is not enough. Being "the only one" or "one of a few" remains extraordinarily difficult. Particular programs and opportunities deserve high priority on college campuses. These encourage and even require peer groups that regularly address the social and academic isolation and the burden of racial insensitivity.

Like Denise, Melissa felt very isolated. She received a four-year LEAD scholarship to a competitive college. LEAD focuses on students of color and first-generation college-goers, and students are selected based on their leadership potential. Although not as all-encompassing as a Posse scholarship, LEAD scholars have regularly scheduled meetings and an advisor for the cohort. "I remember when I arrived on campus, I was so incredibly lonely and scared. But then that same day I had a meeting with the other LEAD scholars. When we all got together, I felt like I could breathe again." Melissa knew she wouldn't necessarily be in classes with all of the other recipients, but at least they would be there if she needed them. She quickly did.

During the first weeks on campus, a girl in one of her classes asked if she could touch her hair. "What am I supposed to say to that? I wanted to yell, 'Hey, I'm not some animal in a zoo! Haven't you ever seen braids on a black person before?!'" The next day she had her cohort meeting, and it was such a relief for her to be able to share that experience with others who had similar stories. "I just hadn't experienced that level of ignorance before," she said. "Sure, in high school there were some issues with race, but we had classes where we could discuss things. That's what Humanities was all about. And even in our art major, we would talk about the kind of music we were performing. Often our repertoire connected to people's struggles throughout history. We sang spirituals. White kids too. I remember when we sang this song, 'Vigala,' from the concentration camps during the Holocaust. Maybe none of us had experienced that, but we understand the pain of seeing your child being taken away and you just want to sing her a lullaby. Singing gave us a way to talk about race, and our differences, but also our similarities." Melissa's story about hair touching was something almost every other girl had experienced. "Why can't there be some kind of orientation about that?" Melissa wondered aloud. "I don't think I would touch a white girl's hair I didn't know and ask why it was so straight."

Melissa became friends with many of the students in the LEAD scholarship cohort; however, she didn't have classes with any of them. Although she enjoyed her classes, they were a constant reminder of her isolation. She was always the only person of color in any class. She brought this discomfort to one of the cohort meetings. "Sometimes I feel nervous about speaking up," she said. "I never felt like that in high school."

A senior told Melissa that in her first year she felt daily microaggressions. "Don't worry about finding a social life in class. Just focus on your studies. That's what you are here for." Melissa nodded and conceded, "I know. I'm going to make it through here. I'm not going to let these people's ignorance throw me. I have a full scholarship so I have to make it through. If it weren't for this group, I don't know what I'd do." The members of the group understood how often Melissa felt disconnected in the college environment. They felt the same way too. "It's as if we don't really belong here," Melissa said. "Like they are doing us a favor letting us come. I'm just as smart as anyone here. Nothing's ever been handed to me." Melissa could always turn to the LEAD cohort where the seniors, in particular, made time for her. They were graduating with honors and going on to jobs and graduate school and they reminded Melissa that three more years really wasn't too long.

Many first-generation college goers feel completely on their own, and race adds another kind of isolation. Melissa found herself comparing notes with Patrick, a BAA classmate who was at a nearby college. Patrick talked about how he experienced race at college where he didn't have anything like LEAD. "You don't have a real community. You don't know where to go. Who are you supposed to ask about stuff that's on your mind?" Patrick talked a lot about how much he loved his classes at college, and even his professors, but he recognized that they didn't really know him. "Not like my teachers in high school knew me." Many researchers write about the importance of knowing students well in order to go beyond racial differences but higher education is not set up that way. Patrick knew that he was considered "extraordinary" at college as a Black male. "That felt really weird. I felt people gave me a lot of room and were sometimes too enthusiastic around me. Like I was a special species or something." He also talked about being nervous around the white women on campus. "So much of the time they all seemed just too into me. But really, a lot of the time, I just was lonely. Like where were my boys?" The idea of a posse as simply a group of people who are sharing similar experiences can acknowledge the racial isolation that students will feel in most campuses. Still, students are expected to figure out on their own whether and how race matters.

AARON'S STORY: STRENGTH IN NUMBERS

Aaron also talks about how lucky he was to have his posse. Aaron was part of the Posse Foundation program that selects students for their leadership potential and sends them to various liberal arts colleges in posses, or groups of ten. That means on any one campus there are forty Posse students (freshmen to seniors). The Posse Foundation's goal is to create an automatic place of belonging. As each freshman cohort enters with three other Posse cohorts already on campus, there is critical mass and support. With such a significant number of students on a chosen campus—all selected for leadership capacity—the foundation's belief is that they and their Posse students can influence debate and make change. By 2020 the Posse Foundation plans to have six thousand students in their network as alumni; their hope is that many of these will take leadership positions as senators, CEOs, successful writers, or lawyers clerking for judges. Posse founder Debbie Bial told me her goal is that "They will begin to make decisions where their voices have traditionally not been represented."[2] The foundation also believes that by working with elite colleges that have traditionally been gatekeepers to opportunity, they will open multiple doors for many young people, particularly those who may not have gained entry without the Posse Foundation's highly competitive admission process.

Posse supports include a pre-college summer program, a Posse advisor, required weekly meetings freshman year and then less often subsequent years. Posse also functions like an elite club through which students have access to mentors to learn about various internships and job opportunities, including summer jobs. Although Posse is a need-blind program, many recipients would never be able to afford private college tuition. Nevertheless, Posse also includes middle and upper income students in each cohort since the criteria for acceptance is leadership potential, not financial need. The goal of each cohort is to represent the diverse demographic of American society.

Even though Aaron said he had done a lot of Posse training with his cohort the summer before freshman year, he still was completely taken aback by the economic and racial disparities as well as the drug use on campus. "I felt like I could get along with almost anyone. I had even gone to a private elementary school. But I guess what you notice when you are eight is really different than when you are eighteen."

Aaron couldn't believe that he was in classes with students who actually had buildings named after their families. "Those were all white kids, but actually, I met different classes of black kids too." He noted that there were the "scholarship black kids," the "partial scholarship black kids," and the "full-paying black kids." What struck Aaron as he tried to make sense of race and class was that, no matter what, race always came first. "Like, we [the scholarship black kids] would make fun of the rich black kids. We thought they were so snotty. They were in fraternities and totally fit into the preppy life of the college. They were on the lacrosse team and the equestrian teams. We'd talk trash about them. They wouldn't really hang with us. But then we heard white kids making fun of them. That kinda brought us all together."

"In my classes I got to study Africana literature and read about social construction of the black male identity in society." He talks about how reading authors like Beverly Daniel Tatum and bell hooks in his race and education class opened his world. "That professor was a black woman and she was, like, amazing. Almost every kid of color on campus wanted to take her course. But that didn't mean that things were easy on campus. I mean I was in a mostly white college in the middle of nowhere." Aaron laughs as he talks about how the different black kids in the various Posse classes would come together to cut one another's hair or to eat snacks sent from home that reminded them of "their food." "We kept thinking how cool it would be if we could start a black barber shop on campus. Not like that would ever happen!"

Aaron recounts his involvement in asking for a cultural center to be dedicated to students of color. The response from white students, and the mostly white administration, was, "We aren't asking for a white hall!" Aaron's group explained that all of the buildings on campus were named for white people and involved the history of white people. "We thought it made sense for people of color to have their space to sit and live together. Just to let down our guard for some of the day." But the administration denied this request. "I was lucky to have my Posse, but even more than the kids, I was lucky to have the mentor I got. And he was a white guy. He really understood what we were fighting for. He was actually on our side." Aaron talks about that relationship as being key to his success in college. This professor met with him weekly his freshman year. By sophomore year it was once a month and then as a junior and senior Posse students choose if you want to meet. For Aaron, this professor, who was also a musician, helped with a myriad of issues that Aaron encountered, including how to get help for depression. But mostly, he opened up the world of music to Aaron, and that kept Aaron occupied during cold and dark winter months. "I was learning about music and connecting that to all sorts of issues with race. And this was from a white professor." Aaron concludes, "So, yeah, Posse helped me through. For sure."

One of the solutions for access to and completion of higher education would be the introduction of more "Posse-like" programs. The answers are not just in writing the college application or understanding how to fill out the financial aid forms. They also lie in having a group to turn to when there are social-emotional issues that arise. Posse-like organizations can also help students navigate the intense class and racial differences on campus. Having a place to go and just relax or commiserate, and then get a pep talk and some possible tools to try, can make the difference between giving up and persisting. Race and privilege can differentiate students in insidious ways. Colleges can gain from vigilance in providing meaningful supports before a student begins to teeter and fall.

LEONI'S STORY: ART AND RACE ON CAMPUS

For Leoni, her racial identity in college plays out this way: "I don't really talk in my classes that have to do with race or other social issues. It's nothing like BAA—there we are expected to talk and disagree and figure things out. The worst part is that this college thinks it's done a really good job with race. Some organizations and classes deal with race. But *real* conversation. That doesn't happen. At least not for me." Leoni doesn't feel much mentoring and support for students of color. You are just expected to figure it out on your own. The fact that the college is located in the heart of a diverse city doesn't seem to matter in terms of how curriculum is presented or discussed.

She struggles with how professors and students turn to her in any discussion about race or ethnicity in classes. She feels that people always defer to her and wait for her to comment first. "It's exhausting to have to represent your race all the time. I don't know very much about African American history. I'm a Latina immigrant!" Leoni senses an assumption on her campus that if you are non-white then you understand both the history of all people of color and you can empathize with all non-white experiences.

Even though her college has a strong arts focus and many majors in the arts, she has not experienced art making at college as a way to cross racial divides. In high school art was a way to "walk in another's shoes." Many assignments were designed to allow students to experience differences as well as similarities across race and social class. But in college, Leoni has not experienced the social justice aspects of art. Art is either considered a singular pursuit or more closely defined as art for art's sake. Art is not something that comes from deep relationships with faculty or students—at least not across racial lines. However, in Leoni's senior year, another student of color, a bi-racial student, directed a play about the experience of being a student of color on the campus. Much like in Kendra's and Aaron's experience, the administration criticized students for portraying a one-sided picture. Nonetheless, the play received enormous accolades from the student body, many professors, and even individual members of the Board of Trustees. Students who worked on the play were asked to present at a full Board meeting where members decided that the college needed an "Office of Student Success" particularly geared toward students of color. Although an AHANA organization (for those of African, Hispanic, Asian, and Native American descent) has been on campus for years, this new office was designed to be pro-active about the needs of students of color. The office also is chartered to work directly with other student organizations on campus so that all students can develop more proficiency and capacity when dealing with peers who come from different backgrounds. "I'm glad it now exists," says Leoni, "for the next generation. But why has it taken so long? I always thought my college was supposed to be really aware of issues of race and class. You'd think colleges would do this better than high schools!"

GENEVRA'S STORY: RACE AND REPRESENTATION

Not addressing race on college campuses does white students a disservice as well. Genevra, a white alumna of BAA, went on to study at a local public university. The campus was pretty diverse, but she found herself unable to find her "bearings," as she called them. "I think I was used to being able to talk about race and class from high school, but in college it was pretty clear that the black kids sat at their table and the white kids at their table." Early on, Genevra tried to sit at the black table but she was quickly shunned by the students and retreated to her own racial group.

"That's not the way it was at BAA. Sure kids of the same races sat to-gether sometimes, but so did all the VAs [Visual Artists] and all the the-ater kids. And we were really mixed. I felt out of place [at college], like I didn't belong there."

This racial divide troubled her, and she wanted to address it. In high school, Genevra felt that her teachers had instilled in her the notion that she had a voice and a responsibility to share her ideas with others. "Sometimes I didn't know what I wanted to say. You know when you are in high school you are kinda uncomfortable about everything. But, at BAA, as one of only two white kids in my class in my major, we learned to talk about race." Genevra recalls a very particular incident that caused tension in the theater department. "We were doing this play and we were doing 'color aware casting.' I had never heard that term. Our teacher ex-plained that when you cast a person of a certain race or color you know the statement you are making. Our play was about urban issues in Amer-ica. The leads were going to be black. That meant that while the white kids could audition for a lead role, we already knew that the leads would be black or brown."

While Genevra's recollection of the color-aware casting incident was mostly positive, I remember having to defend the decision to practically every white theater parent in all grades. They were furious that their stu-dent had been told that they could audition but wouldn't be cast as a lead. I asked if Genevra remembered their objections. "How will you get the experience you need to audition for college?" they said. Genevra tried to explain that it was just one show and she would have other opportunities. Genevra may not have understood all the particulars of the decision, but says she knew she was part of something important. "We were having an important conversation, and that was good, even if some people had their feelings hurt." Genevra also thought that the parents' negative reactions fueled the student commitment to color-aware casting.

In college Genevra discovered a theater department, but it put on very few shows that raised racial issues in productive or insightful ways. "I felt like I was wasting my time there. I had been trained to use my art to think through and be provocative about issues of our time and our community, but at my college we were doing pretty obscure stuff that didn't seem very relevant to me." The theater faculty at her college was overwhelmingly white and chose plays with little to no bearing on the issues that were erupting on campuses throughout the country. Genevra spoke to her dean about choices the department made. "I wanted the dean to see that these kinds of 'white bread' plays were actually hurting us," she said. "We needed to use our art to make our voices heard. We needed to use art to help one another see and imagine a different kind of society. We needed theater to make a stand."

Nothing changed in the theater department, but in her African American history classes Genevra began to study more about race and racism, social class, and privilege. "I began to learn about how I benefit on a daily basis from white privilege." She also thought about her pre-dominantly white neighborhood in Boston, and all the people she knew that benefitted from their privilege. "I saw that many people I knew and loved were determined to live an unexamined life. It was just easier that way for them." Genevra ended up leaving college for a few years to start a theater and film company with a friend from high school. The company produced work that focused on current issues as well as women's empowerment. "I began to think about what it would be like if all high school and college kids had to learn about what it's like to be followed home as a woman, or what it's like to be stopped by a police officer just because you are black?" As Genevra thought about her friends in college, she realized just how disconnected they were from the experiences of others. "If we could really learn, in some kind of experiential way, what it's like to come from another background or race or culture, we would be so much better equipped to live in this world. But none of that is val-ued in school. College is about how you do as an individual and how you do compared to others. But that won't help make this a better world." Although Genevra eventually received her degree, she has not lost her anger about the ways that race was ignored at college.

Eric, a BAA alumnus, talks about growing up in a predominantly white and middle-class neighborhood in Boston. "BAA was really the first time that I thought about what it means to come from some place where you don't have two parents at home, one of whom can always make a nutritious dinner or snack." He continues, "At BAA there was so much diversity. I learned about empathy there." He talks about admir-ing classmates who had to work over twenty hours a week, and practice their art and do homework. "I just had a job on Saturdays. And that was because I wanted a job, not because I needed a job to support my family." Eric emphasizes that he had grown up with people "pretty much like me—more affluent and white. At BAA we learned to talk with one another about our differences and to have meaningful conversation that actually brought us closer." When I asked how this skill transferred to college, Eric said with a sigh, "College wasn't diverse at all. I could never really figure out how to engage with the few kids of color there. Even though I identified as an urban kid, it wasn't the same, and college wasn't set up to bring diverse people together. It just wasn't important."

Obama's election may have been historic but certainly did not herald a post-racial society. Evidence of this festers in colleges and universities and how they respond in a systemic way to the experiences of students like Kendra, Denise, Melissa, Pat, Aaron, Leoni, Genevra, and Eric.

First of all, as long as their stories are seen as individual as opposed to representative of the larger issues in higher education, the less likely it is that there will be true changes on campuses. College is hard for most young people. Add racial isolation and issues of economics and social class and the experience can be overwhelming.

I invite colleges and universities to examine such research along with the stories of students like mine to help improve both student experiences and the success of their institutions. My students are indicative of a growing norm. An infusion of new resources for a student success office or a diversity director and staff may be a tough order for campuses that have neither, but without these structures, all students suffer and colleges lose ground. Diversity and inclusion are crucial values for our society—especially given the ugly politics we are experiencing today. How diversity is included—how students feel they belong—is the simple key to success. Too many people in our country are growing up in complete racial and socioeconomic isolation. Consider how this reality feeds our economic and social divide: In a recent study at Brandeis University, "just 21 percent of federally subsidized [housing] units in Eastern Massachusetts are in so-called high-opportunity neighborhoods, with ready access to jobs, healthy food and quality schools."[3] This means nearly 80 percent of subsidized housing is in poor neighborhoods.

Without opportunities to cross boundaries, we have little chance to know and understand people from different backgrounds. This is a danger to avoid in colleges, not one to mimic.

HIGH SCHOOL: LIVING AN ANTIRACIST AGENDA

What college leaders should do in *receiving* students could better mirror our preparation in *sending* students to college. Yet high schools themselves can also benefit from the learning offered by these BAA alumni experiences. Our students, both white and of color, deserve to be prepared to face the myriad ways that race matters on college campuses, especially those enrolling in majority-white schools.

The BAA curriculum heralds a student's ability to interrogate race, ethnicity, social class, and language of origin. BAA lives actively as an antiracist institution. Much of the curriculum focuses on the history of oppressed people in the United States. The central question in sophomore humanities class is "Who has power in America and why?" Students research the experiences of a variety of Americans through multiple lenses, such as race, gender, social class, and citizenship status. Rigorous sequential study in an arts discipline, often from an antiracist perspective, provides students with additional skills. Many of the plays we present, the music we sing, even the artists we study have a strong social justice emphasis. Our students become versatile in discussing issues (with evidence from texts) that are often polarizing to others. Continual discussion among the faculty highlights how and whether pedagogy and curriculum are focused on engaging all students, and specifically students of color who are in the majority. During my tenure, the faculty was approximately 50 percent teachers of color. Many were first-generation college graduates. Many had been shaped by fights against racial, linguistic, gender, and class injustices. They could recollect and discuss their own experiences with microaggressions in college and in life.

As the leader of BAA, and a white woman from another era of social movements in this country, I was inclined to support my students' exploration and indignations about social and racial injustice. Not until I listened to their experiences post high school, did I begin to consider that my enthusiasm and inclinations lacked an analysis of power. I hadn't deeply considered how exhausting it was for Aaron and others to keep fighting "against the man," or the power structure at his college.

My interviews with alumni also led me to talk to some of their parents. One African American parent said to me as we celebrated her daughter's graduation from college: "Thank goodness she didn't get picked off by all her protesting." She was referencing her child's learning about social movements and racial justice in high school. Yet in a predominantly white institution, she wanted her child to have enough sense not to get kicked out by *talking race*. "I just wanted her to get her degree, and I was afraid that with all that organizing they'd find a reason not to let her graduate." I needed to hear this. As a white woman and college activist in the 1970s at a large public university, I never had to think about any risk to my own graduation.

Today, over half of our students in American public schools are of color. Studies tell us that young students of color experience and perceive the structures in American society and education as rigged against them. This is especially true for African American males,[4] who are typically overrepresented on the bottom rung of the achievement ladders on most measures. African American males are more likely to be suspended or expelled. They are more likely to be tracked into remedial courses and absent from honors courses. Graduation rates from both high school and college for young men of color are below white males. Prison rates are so egregious that the term "cradle-to-prison pipeline" was coined to describe the phenomenon. As an educator and institutional leader, I believe that full engagement in antiracist education, with all faculty and staff and at all levels of the education system, develops communities where young people can begin to defy these odds in greater numbers. Consider how schools use language (which is a good indicator of practice) to define themselves: "Our kids struggle with lots of tough home situations . . ." or "Our population of kids hasn't had many opportunities . . ." or "Well, you know our kids . . ." Though these phrases may come from good intentions, they rarely begin with strengths, or create helpful impact. Using this focus to explain low achievement rather than examining our own instructional practices sets up a deficit model of education. The challenge is to become skilled in an antiracist curriculum without ignoring or excusing external factors. This means personal and professional responsibility to meet the needs of struggling students of color while also recognizing the context of students and families. This is not easy. Yet how we prepare our students before leaving high school, and how colleges prepare to receive them, can open a wide world of potential for education in America.

INDIVIDUAL PROFESSIONALS: FINDING THE COURAGE WITHIN

Even as I argue about the urgency for colleges to further support a more diverse student body, I reflect on another equally complex theme: how to better prepare K–12 educators to talk and teach about race. We must demand and build in time to give educators the tools and practice to teach an effective antiracist pedagogy.

Growing up in Cambridge, Massachusetts, I witnessed the violent struggles to desegregate the Boston Public Schools in the 1970s. I then became a bilingual teacher in Boston five years after court-ordered desegregation. These experiences gave me a very particular commitment to engaging in antiracist education for teachers.

When I opened BAA in 1998 as the founding headmaster, one of the school's founding presidents said to me, "Boston doesn't have to just be known as one of the most racist cities in America. We can overcome our ugly history of segregation and desegregation battles. BAA can move us forward to a new era where, through immersive experiences in the arts, students will learn tolerance and a true appreciation of differences of all kinds." In 1998, those were aspirational words. Words of hope. Today, they are words that remind me how critical antiracist education is with the adults in our school.

The book *Courageous Conversations* has been a successful starting point to engage educators, and even students, in rethinking how to approach institutionalized racism and ever-growing racial and socioeconomic opportunity gaps in our country. The authors, Glenn Singleton and Curtis Linton, write, "Anti-racism can be defined as conscious and deliberate efforts to challenge the impact and perpetuation of institutional White racial power, presence, and privilege."[5] Their examination of institutionalized white racism is not viewed as being against white people but rather in terms of how all races can gain the same access and privileges that "white people tend to demand, to feel entitled to, and to take for granted. Anti-racism means working toward a realization of the ideals that the United States professes are true for all citizens."[6]

Using this definition and this text, I cofacilitated a series of professional development workshops for a racially mixed group of emerging teacher-leaders.[7] Agreement on the definition was not easy, especially on singling out white people. All the participants had been classroom teachers for at least five years and came from urban schools. This professional development was part of their work toward administrative licensure to become principals. Over our twelve weeks together, we established a level of trust so that everyone felt fairly safe speaking in the group.

Daphne, a white teacher, shared a previous experience talking about race in a mixed group. "It was in college, in a class I took about power, race, and language. No matter what we talked about, I always left class feeling badly about being white. I'm not a bad person and I rarely, if ever, come from a place of hate. But the discussion of whiteness in these conversations was just so uncomfortable for me."

Stephen, another white teacher, concurred with Daphne. "I truly believe that race only matters if you want it to. In my school, I don't think we are helping our students when the conversation turns 'racial.' Also, I always chafe at the fact that while all groups can show prejudice, only white people are called racist."

Another member of the group, Angela, an African American teacher, countered, "As a person of color, I'm constantly aware of race. It's not something I can turn on or off like you can as white people. It's who I am and it's who my students are. We do them a disservice by not discussing race."

Stephen insisted that the continuing focus on race in school did his students of color a disservice. "It causes them to think about themselves as less than others. We need to ensure that all kids are learning, and not keep harping on the achievement gap and race." This comment elicited strong reactions from teachers across race, especially from Barry, an African American who sighed audibly: "Our children know about race and inequity whether you want to try and keep it away or not. The question is this: How can we assure that white teachers, who actually are in the majority in most of our urban schools, learn to help our students acquire the race skills that they need?" He then elaborated on prejudice and racism: "We cannot talk about white people having experienced *institutionalized racism*. How is that different from prejudice? You may have experienced prejudice. But you have not experienced institutionalized racism. As a white person, you cannot. Institutionalized racism is about power. White people in this country still have the power."

This conversation about definitions was an important starting point. Barry had brought an illustration that was familiar to some members of the group to help understand the difference between equity and equality.[8] The illustration is two images of three young people of different heights standing on stools of equal height while watching a baseball game from behind a fence. In the first image, the tallest child can easily see over the fence to enjoy the game; the second tallest can also see over the fence, but just barely; the third child, who is the smallest, cannot see over the fence at all. However, in the second image, the tallest has given his stool to the shortest child, and now everyone can enjoy the game. Now the shortest child has two stools that stack one on top of the other. The middle child has the original single stool, and the tallest child has no stool at all. Barry summarized, "So this helps us see that in order to bring equality to the playing field, equity [or the process of action] needed to change in terms of who gets a stool, and of what height."

Stephen spoke after a long pause. We let the pause last, though it was an uncomfortable moment for us as facilitators. "I get how this stool thing works for watching a baseball game. I really do. But what does it mean when we bring this into schools? What does this mean for a student ten years from now?" Stephen asked. "Will they always expect that extra help? Will it become an excuse? A crutch?"

Barry spoke slowly and firmly. "I benefited from that extra support. It allowed me to catch up and learn about self-advocacy. I think it positively shaped me, and sensitized me to the many different needs of young people across race and other backgrounds. I don't see myself, today, needing extra support, do you?" The question hung in the air. Part of what we learn in this work is to expect non-closure and discomfort.

Then Kim spoke. She had been quiet during this entire interchange and during many of our sessions. She began, "I agree that this image is helpful. And this picture helps us see things from a different perspective.

But, it's not just white people who get uncomfortable talking about race. As an Asian American female, I find this kind of discussion very hard. In my last school we did a lot of work on diversity that really hurt the relationships among the adults. We had a great community before we began that work, but by digging in and looking so closely at each other and our biases, it really rocked the boat and brought up stuff that we couldn't put away. I'm very hesitant about engaging in this kind of talk."

Angela listened attentively to Kim. "Maybe the facilitation was bad, but we have to be able to talk and critique one another in schools—and about topics that are hard to discuss—like race. I hate to bring [President George W.] Bush into the conversation, but I agreed with him when he talked about the 'soft bigotry of low expectations.' With too many of my colleagues, particularly my white colleagues, I see teachers who just don't get that you have to have high expectations and not feel sorry for kids. I was raised in poverty and I made it, and that's what I want for all the kids I teach. You gotta stop making excuses for black and brown kids." A wave of "amens" moved through the group.

This type of remark is often at one end of the "courageous conversations" spectrum. At the other end is denial that talking about race matters. Both of these positions tend to shut down productive conversations that can actually help kids. Moreover, it is not just a "white" and "black" issue when many different ethnic, racial, biracial, and cultural groups are represented. Nonetheless, since white people have been the dominant group in the United States historically, the role of whiteness in discussions of race is imperative to understand. I've had many white students, and white teachers, from poor backgrounds who insisted that they, like their counterparts of color, had experienced degradation, lack of opportunities, and even prejudice. But we need teachers, like Stephen, to explain how these experiences, while insulting and hurtful, are not the same as institutionalized racism.

Our work together brought revelatory moments. Katy, another white teacher in the group, realized she used the word "chatty" to describe white girls misbehaving in class, while for boys of color demonstrating the same behavior she used "disruptive." Kim nodded. "So often we talk about Asians as the model minority. We expect Asian students to be good students. That's a lot of pressure too."

In working with this group of teachers, I kept returning to the stories my alumni had shared with me. To help them understand these student experiences, I included the classic 1989 work of antiracist educator Peggy McIntosh, "White Privilege: Unpacking the Invisible Knapsack":

> I think whites are carefully taught not to recognize white privilege, as males are taught not to recognize male privilege. . . . I have come to see white privilege as an invisible package of unearned assets that I can count on cashing in each day, but about which I was "meant" to remain oblivious. White privilege is like an invisible weightless knapsack of special provisions, maps, passports, codebooks, visas, clothes, tools, and blank checks.[9]

McIntosh then lists fifty ways or conditions that allow her white privilege. She urges us to spend time unpacking what these privileges mean in daily life. For example, "I can go shopping alone most of the time, pretty well assured I will not be followed or harassed." Or, "I can, if I wish, arrange to be in the company of people of my race most of the time."

This article led to an important conversation about allied behavior. Stephen brought in a video for us to watch, which he had found on Facebook. In it, educator and author Joy Angela DeGruy recounts her experience shopping at a Safeway grocery story with her sister-in-law, Kathleen, who could pass as white, yet is half black.[10] The cashier chats with Kathleen pleasantly while she pays for her groceries with a check. When Joy takes out her checkbook to pay for her groceries, the cashier asks for two forms of identification. Both Joy and her ten-year-old daughter are surprised. But Joy doesn't want to protest and play "the angry black woman," so she just gives the cashier two forms of ID. At that point, the cashier takes out a large book that lists the "bad check people" and slowly starts looking for Joy's name. Joy's daughter asks, with tears in her eyes, "Why is she doing this to us, Mommy?" Kathleen intervenes, "What are you doing? You didn't ask me for ID!" The cashier says, "It's standard policy." Two elderly people waiting in line behind Joy ask to speak to the manager. "This is not standard policy. This is harassment," they say.

The point of the story is not necessarily the apparent racial discrimination but rather that Kathleen used her white privilege as allied behavior and intervened to prevent the situation from escalating, as did the two elderly white people. That was what Stephen wanted to discuss. This video made him think about his role in talking about race and racism and how he can be an ally too. If these workshops allow teachers to move along a continuum of antiracist or "allied" actions, we have more possibilities to bring equity to our schools and classrooms.

While antiracist work has no quick fixes, these discussions can have a direct and practical impact on teacher practice. Daphne described the guilt that her colleagues feel about the achievement gap (often defined as the differences on test scores between white and Asian students and black and Latino students). "By third grade we see the gaps. We are all working so hard. And our kids and families love us. Our kids do just great work—wonderful projects. Then, we get their scores back. And there it is in our faces, again. Our white, Asian and middle-class students score better than our poorer students and our students of color. Our principal wants us to dig more into the data, but we don't want to be a school where race matters. We are a school where kids matter."

Daphne explains the faculty's ongoing work to examine their practices and the achievement gap. "We read Claude Steele's *Whistling Vivaldi* about 'how stereotypes affect us and what we can do.' We've always had focus on equity and diversity, and teachers regularly examined their practices and assumptions about teaching, learning, and success for all students. But when the test scores came back, it felt to us like nothing had changed." They had studied, talked, and even tried some different policies—such as no homework up through fifth grade. But the test results seemed to defy any new practices.

Our group used Daphne's dilemma as a collective problem to solve. One suggestion involved after-school. The more middle-class students paid for an after-school program at the school. Other students, with less means, went to free after-school programs elsewhere with few links to their classroom activities. Once this was discovered, some teachers visited the free after-school program to provide curriculum overviews about classroom skills and activities. Just this small intervention made a positive difference.

A different stance of strict rules, rigor, and relentless high expectations often translates into a "no-excuses" kind of curriculum devoid of any opportunity to integrate the study of race and class. We need to meld these often opposing stances. Race, along with discussions of socioeconomic class, culture, language, and gender, should be a topic of serious and meaningful inquiry and debate in all schools. We can maintain high expectations for achievement while including thoughtful and purposeful discussions about equity—a vital component to prepare all students to enter a diverse world. Most importantly, this is ongoing work, not simply once-a-year professional development.

Singleton and Linton integrate the examination of data along with carefully calibrated inquiry and effective antiracist readings and exercises. Teachers in all schools need enough professional development time to work carefully and collaboratively through books like *Courageous Conversations* and McIntosh's knapsack. If our students are better prepared in high school then college will not be such a shock.

While preparing this chapter, I read some of the passages to students in a college class on education. Later, one of the students, a young white sophomore named Caitlin, asked if she could interview me for a piece she was writing for the college newspaper. She echoed many of the forms of white privilege that Peggy McIntosh wrote about almost thirty years ago. "You can grow up and not see inequality. I lived in a completely white world. Not until I came to college did I begin to understand the difference between equity and inequality. I am trying to figure out how it's possible that in this country so many people grow up like me, and what I can do about that. It has to do with money, too. My high school had lots of funding. And scholarships for college were barely talked about, except for merit scholarships. Now I've listened to your students' stories and realize that issues of race and social class really do matter."

So why is this chapter titled "Race Doesn't Matter"? I am responding to an attitude in this country that "just prove yourself to be worthy" is all that's needed in life. We see this attitude in our highest courts when voting rights legislation is overturned. We see this in the continual objections to affirmative action in higher education admissions or in exam school selection in the Boston Public Schools. If we allow an assumption like "race doesn't matter" to prevail, racial issues can be conveniently explained or excused as singular matters to be solved by individual intervention. Singular responses allow us to avoid the actions needed for racial and socio-economic equity and a path toward a healthy and vibrant society and economy.

Students like Caitlin need earlier exposure to the inequities in our society. When young people have such limited experiences, then it is hard to combat ignorance and create the conditions for change. If we embrace antiracist education as a core component of our work, then our students will develop more sophisticated skills and more resilience to confront racism in all forms. When we engage in this complex work with our students our entire society will benefit. The loss of lives, the enormity of the racial achievement gap, the lack of understanding about racial, ethnic, religious, and gender differences all undermine our society in grievous ways.

Beginning nationally in early elementary school, curricula must include consistent study and exposure to issues of racial injustice so that more young people learn to talk and think critically about racial justice. Our teachers, too, must be versatile in guiding conversations with young people. Finally, our colleges and universities have much to learn simply from the uplifting initiatives like LEAD and Posse, and the unrealized ability of schools to develop those programs into institution-wide practice. We know that race matters deeply for young people and adults. Structural inequality and institutionalized racism are realities in this country. We cannot diminish their impact unless we confront their existence. Teaching about race is *the* essential first step. This takes practice, comfort with discomfort, a willingness to accept our own bias, and the ability to imagine a more just world.

CHAPTER THREE

"Just Work Harder"

Having worked in public education for four decades, I have seen education trends come and go. "Open classrooms" were all the buzz when I began teaching. There were few physical dividers, and children could migrate to areas of the classroom that interested them. At different times in my career, cooperative learning has battled for airtime with collaborative learning. There have been entire books written about which strategy best supports reading comprehension. I have talked with my colleagues in educational psychology about what a strong hold "right brain and left brain teaching" had on generations of teachers, even though research has demonstrated there is no such thing. Portfolio assessment replaced multiple-choice "bubble tests" for a short while; multicultural education has given way to culturally responsive teaching. The list goes on and on. My point is this: social, cultural, and political changes influence education trends. Since the 1990s, in urban education there has been a strong emphasis on lifting low expectations and getting students to work harder (Jeff Howard's Efficacy Institute is one example[1]). The focus today continues in that vein. We tell students that if they work harder, they will succeed. My sense is that the latest incarnation of this axiom is the "let's get gritty" call to action. "Grit" puts the focus on student initiative, often ignoring social and economic factors that can undermine even the best of efforts.

For the last decade or so, grit has been the holy grail for educators trying to improve their students' performance: "If we could just teach them to be grittier"; "If they just understood that persistence pays off"; "If we could only get them to realize that determination leads to success." All of these aspirations are valid. It is true that you need grit, persistence, and determination to do well in school and in life. It is, of course, true that that these attributes will help young people navigate obstacles and perhaps even find success in college and beyond. But what about the structural barriers that low-income and black and brown students have to navigate every day? All this talk of grit seems to sidestep the real issue: there are institutional inequities embedded within American education. The assumption "You just have to work hard" is based on the story of the "underdog" who miraculously "makes it" and thus attains almost mythic status in our society. For many middle- and upper-class Americans, hard work (and lots of support) may indeed get them to the next level, even if obstacles are put in their way. The same is not generally true for poor people. It's not that grit is unimportant; it's just not sufficient. It certainly is not the holy grail that it has been cracked up to be, and it certainly is not the cure-all it has been portrayed as in so much education literature.

In this chapter, I examine stories of BAA alums who had a tremendous amount of grit but also faced enormous institutional barriers that confounded their success beyond high school. My intent is to learn from their stories so that educators can put grit in its proper place: as an important but not sufficient indicator of whether kids will succeed. Sure, hard work might get you further than others in your group or cohort. Working hard might get you a full-time job with benefits while your peers are working three part-time jobs just to get by. But if the end game is a baccalaureate degree or professional status, working hard will get you only so far.

What all the talk about grit seems to miss is the importance of putting children's experiences front and center. In other words, when the emphasis on grit ends up as stand-alone pedagogy, the context of students' life and family circumstances is ignored. We are fast becoming a majority-minority country, and "minority" children are fast becoming the majority in US public schools. Their experiences and the ways they and their families navigate the education system serve to educate us all. My hope is that the students profiled in this chapter, who show no lack of grit, will instruct us in ways that help educators recognize and fight against structural inequities that work against success.

ROSA: CONTEXT MATTERS

I always loved school as a child. I loved my teachers. I loved learning. I worked hard. When I became a teacher, I wanted to instill that same love of learning and work ethic in my students.

In the urban public middle school where I first taught in the 1970s, the curriculum and support that I had enjoyed in my K–12 experiences was almost non-existent. The motto was clear: work hard and you will have a chance at success. However, the deck was stacked against many of my students. Even those who did exactly what their teachers said, and followed all the rules, still had a lower chance of success than their middle-class peers. One talented student named Rosa comes to mind. Given all of the accolades she got in middle school, we were confident she would go on to college. With the drive, the passion, and the skills to be successful, she would be the first high school graduate in her family. Her parents had migrated from Puerto Rico and neither had finished middle school. Rosa, a second language learner, didn't get the requisite test scores for Boston's exam schools. She ended up at a large district high school where she was part of a freshman class of five hundred. Her high school felt chaotic and alienating to her, and her guidance counselor had over three hundred students to advise. Even though Rosa tried to switch into college-prep classes, she was told she had to stay in her English as a Second Language classes until she had advanced enough. She knew that meant she was falling behind in other subjects (since she was tracked into an ESL cohort which didn't give her access to a competitive high school curriculum), and so she petitioned for changes, but no one paid much attention to her. I tried to intervene, but my requests also fell on deaf ears. "We can't just switch her into those classes because her English isn't strong enough. You don't want her to fail, do you?" Both Rosa and I were convinced that even though her English test results were low, she could do the work, especially in math and science classes that were less language dependent. But we couldn't convince the 'establishment.' I stayed in touch with Rosa, even tutoring her regularly, hoping that the following year she would be able to advance more rapidly.

Learning English was not Rosa's only obstacle. Gang violence was on the rise and had permeated the school. Rosa's boyfriend was nominally involved in a gang "for his own protection," he said. Rosa began to get drawn in as well. She had little support for "being smart." Rosa wasn't my only student from that first group who got lost in the transition from middle to high school. So many of my "smart" students never graduated from high school. Some were pulled out of school on a regular basis to translate for parents who needed them for appointments with various city and state agencies. Sometimes, students were late to school because they had to help younger siblings get on the bus since their parents were working two and three jobs. At times, the demands of younger siblings or emergencies of an infirm relative created havoc in my students' lives. Some were overwhelmed by the rising neighborhood crime and violence. Many students lost relatives to either gang-related violence, AIDS, or crack/cocaine. Other students couldn't find the connections between school and the struggles of their own home or community.

Out of this devastating era in American cities, a few students became the "miracles" of their neighborhood. No one really talked about how these miracles occurred: perhaps there was a teacher or a relative who just never let go, or a special intervention program, or the stars just aligned and things worked out. This select few were the archetype—the evidence that if you worked hard, you will succeed. They were living proof that education could be the antidote to poverty. These exceptions became the totems of the establishment, used as evidence that hard work is enough to succeed. For me, however, Rosa's struggle served as a wake-up call and set me on a journey to try to more accurately understand the role of context in my students' lives. Just working hard is not enough. Smart, motivated Rosa, who could have been one of those exceptions, did not finish high school.

THE SEDUCTIVENESS OF GRIT

Years after teaching Rosa, a book deeply challenged my thinking: *How Children Succeed*, by Paul Tough.[2] Tough's discussion of how character traits might be taught and valued in schools made me wonder if there was something we hadn't been doing all these years. I remembered the *character education* curriculum of the 1980s that came and went like so many other short-lived trends in the field, but this seemed different. Might some panacea ensure my students' success? Tough recounts stories and research about seven character traits that might positively change outcomes for young people. Grit, zest, self-control, social intelligence, optimism, curiosity, and conscientiousness came to be part of the discourse of educational reform. The genesis of "grit" in the psychological literature caught my attention as I reflected on early teaching experiences, especially with students like Rosa. Could their outcome have been different had we been more conversant with this emerging idea? And could an understanding of grit have helped Rosa rise above her circumstances? I am just not sure.

Even before Tough's book, psychologist Angela Duckworth and her colleagues engaged in research that would codify the term "grit" in the education literature. She and colleagues studied why some cadets at West Point dropped out and others stayed on after their first difficult summer of training. They developed a scale to measure grit and a definition that included "not just having resilience in the face of failure, but also having deep commitments that you remain loyal to over many years."[3] In reflecting on the study of the cadets, Duckworth says, "Woody Allen once quipped that 80 percent of success in life is just showing up. Well, it looks like grit is one thing that determines who shows up. We've seen echoes of our West Point findings in studies of many other groups, such as National Spelling Bee contestants, and first-year teachers in tough schools. Grit predicts success over and beyond talent. When you consider individuals of equal talent, the grittier ones do better. Grit is not just about perseverance over time, but also passion over time."[4] Although I heartily agreed, I was uncomfortable with how the thinking around grit quickly translated into classroom practices.

A new breed of education reformers soon embraced Duckworth's theories and adopted them in what became known as the "no excuses" pedagogy. These "reformers" (my quotation marks here indicate my discomfort with this approach, even though I respect and admire many individuals in this arena) believed that by working harder, more efficiently, and more independently of bureaucracy, they could create better outcomes for young people. The "no excuses" mantra expressed the belief that high achievement was within reach of all students if they had the schools they deserved and teachers who would challenge and support them. With these elements in place, nothing would stop marginalized students—not poverty, not family trauma, not health or mental health issues, not speaking a language other than English, having special needs, or being undocumented. The Knowledge Is Power Program (KIPP) was the first in a chain of charter schools to espouse the "no excuses" rhetoric. The rhetoric quickly became synonymous with a growing movement called "no excuses schools." Early on, KIPP generated persuasive student-achievement results. "No excuses" charter schools began to capture the imagination and enthusiasm of many in the education-policy and philanthropic communities. *Washington Post* education reporter Jay Mathews wrote a popular book praising the early gains of KIPP schools.[5] Suddenly, the new truth was that strict discipline alongside an emphasis on teacher quality could level the playing field between poor and minority youth and middle-class and white students.

Teach for America was also born from this conviction. I heard Wendy Kopp speak in 1990 as she was forming TFA after graduating from Princeton, and I was excited by how she might inspire a new generation to enter teaching. I had been a teacher for about twelve years by then, and I knew we needed to grow our ranks. Her argument was similar: if you just hire bright, well-intentioned young people to work in high-poverty schools, thereby circumventing educators who don't believe in high standards or doing whatever it takes, these young, energetic teachers will positively affect the educational outcomes of their students. (Later TFA claimed that they were not as interested in developing a teacher-preparation program to change educational outcomes as in creating leaders and advocates for improved public education.)[6] An entire education-reform movement began to embrace the notion that low standards and low expectations by teachers were responsible for low outcomes for poor and minority children. In addition to adding programs like Teach for America, more testing and stricter accountability measures were incorporated into the requirements of teachers and schools.

The idea of grit was part of the DNA of this movement, and as its inclusion in classroom teaching became commonplace, external factors such as poverty and institutionalized racism became taboo explanations as root causes for low achievement. They were seen as excuses for lazy teachers, administrators, and even students who weren't working hard enough. Others believed that unions and bloated bureaucracies were also to blame for poor student performance. The "no excuses" approach became a panacea, and a much less expensive alternative to investing in antipoverty programs like Head Start or Job Corps.

Student behavior and discipline were already KIPP cornerstones. KIPP piloted the SLANT behavior system: Sit Up, Listen, Ask questions, Nod [at the speaker], and Track [the person talking]. SLANT reflected the desire to teach "code switching." Simply put, schools would teach young people behaviors that were deemed successful in the professional world but might not be common in their neighborhoods or even homes. In other words, KIPPsters (a term sometimes used to refer to students at KIPP schools) might say, "In order to succeed in the dominant culture, you need to know how to do these things. It's what's expected. It's professional behavior. It's what colleges expect." Demonstrating grit, teaching how to be "gritty," quickly became a natural part of the nomenclature in many KIPP and other no-excuses schools. The premise: keep students focused on a task in front of them and control their levels of distraction and you could increase their grit indicators. (Duckworth developed a way to measure for grit, including gauging the ability to focus on goals, finish projects, and overcome setbacks.)[7] Duckworth's experiments showed that praising students for doing something that they felt was difficult, and not necessarily enjoyable, for example, completing homework, studying, or practicing, could lead them to become grittier.[8]

Author Paul Tough also chronicles how two academic leaders came together to experiment with how to teach character traits like grit. Exploring the alliance between David Levin, cofounder of KIPP, and Dominic Randolph, principal of Riverdale Country Day School, a private independent day school in New York (and Levin's alma mater), Tough found the differences in approaches and conclusions to be stark. SLANT, which was being implemented at KIPP, was anathema at Riverdale, where students might commonly sit hunched in a chair or slouch back, or let their hair fall over their eyes and appear *not* to be listening to a classmate or teacher. This was tolerated and accepted. For students already part of the dominant culture, chewing gum or having an untucked shirt did not equate with bad behavior or bad character. Tough describes these differences. He quotes a Riverdale guidance counselor who says, "Here, you can sit in a ball in your chair and no one cares. We don't care if you lie on the floor."[9] The same is not true for KIPP or other "no excuses" schools. In this world, if you are poor, black, or brown, you must adhere to a rigid behavior code as the entrée into success. Unlike their middle-class white counterparts, low-income children or black and brown children seldom are given liberty to just be themselves in educational settings. And this is particularly true when being yourself doesn't align with expectations and presumed normative attitudes and behaviors that teachers have come to expect. Therefore, too often, because the expectations of poor children and children of color are so low, they must "appear" a certain way, especially in "no excuses" schools and classrooms, to receive the respect of the educators.

KIPP and other "no excuses" school models have commitments or contracts that parents, students, and teachers must sign. An example for students is the vow "I will always behave so as to protect the safety, interest, and rights of all individuals in the classroom. This also means that I will always listen to my KIPP teammates and give everyone my respect." Another describes telling the truth to teachers and accepting responsibility for one's actions. These commitments don't seem unreasonable, but the last statement gives me pause: "Failure to adhere to these commitments can cause me to lose various KIPP privileges and can lead to returning to my home school."

I've worked in public schools for almost forty years and I am familiar with codes of discipline, but I have never seen a code that could cause removal of a student from the school for anything less than egregious, inflammatory behavior. I wonder about a system that assumes a "home" school is where you go when you've been expelled. The home school is often in a student's neighborhood and embedded in the culture of that particular socioeconomic, linguistic, and racial community. Imagine the subliminal implications of "home" as a threat, of "home" as less than the "no excuses" school. Imagine being told that if you have failed at displaying enough grit, you will be returned to an educational setting in which the chances for success will not exist in your future.

My problem with the grit approach is that it has taken on an importance far out of proportion to the many other traits that may be just as critical for student development and success. Furthermore, the extensive focus on grit in schools has often been criticized for being culturally insensitive to the backgrounds of many students.[10] The no-excuses movement has "unabashedly instructed and obliged students and families of color to act according to middle-class, White norms."[11] Author and educator Chris Emdin goes further by comparing some of the no-excuses discipline tactics to police brutality. "When I see young people who are not allowed to express their culture or use their voice, or have to control their physical body in a certain way to make their teacher feel more comfortable, I see those acts as violence against students. Those are not physical acts of violence, but violence to their spirit, on their soul, and on their personhood, and it robs them of joy."[12] Many educators argue for teaching students through a lens of critical pedagogy. What this means in practice is that teachers need to help students of color embrace their own powerful identities and backgrounds as part of their educational journey, and from there assist them in navigating a racist and oppressive society.

GRIT AND ITS DISCONTENTS

To see for myself how grit was taught and how these no-excuses traits had become embedded, I visited a number of schools. In one school, the hallways proudly displayed pictures of students with words like "grit" underneath the student's profile: "Tony showed grit on 2/24 when he finished all his homework on time." Another poster was a picture of a young girl with this written below: "Darlene demonstrated conscientiousness and grit on 3/16 when she helped her group finish their presentation." Many posters used the acronym TIGER, which stands for Teamwork, Integrity, Grit, Engagement, and Respect. These are clearly the values (and rules) of the school. A number of the faculty and staff members wore shirts emblazoned with GRIT on the front and the school's name on the back. Many signs reminded students to SLANT.

In some of my classroom visits, these words were used regularly in teachers' pedagogy. Grit took center stage everywhere. I counted fifteen repetitions of a fourth-grade math teacher saying to students, "Good use of grit!" or "That was a very gritty response." Throughout the exchanges, the decibel level of the teacher's voice was very high, almost shouting. In lots of call-and-response activities, the teacher flung out questions and students responded in unison in chants or raps (also very loudly). Such mnemonic devices can be very effective for memorization, and have become associated with how to help children develop grit, but I'm not sure that shouting is a requirement. A lot of finger snapping showed that students had understood a concept, and there was a lot of finger wiggling when a student got an answer right. "Let's show Sonya some love!" the teacher said after she went up to the board, and everyone wiggled their fingers at her. In another instance, the teacher reminded the class to practice SLANT-ing. "You shouldn't need any reminders at this point in the year, but I still see students who are not tracking the speaker." These devices were part of helping students stay focused on the task at hand and were presumably intended to help them "get grittier."

I watched this class during dismissal as they lined up quietly and walked quietly through the hall. Teachers were stationed at various intervals throughout the hallway. One young white woman repeatedly interrupted the flow by issuing a one-word command as the students passed. I didn't quite grasp the word until I saw students stepping out of line and heading to the back as they quickly tucked in their shirts and tightened their belts. They then rejoined the line to enter their next classroom. One teacher stood at the door to his classroom and shook the hands of students as they entered, demanding with his clear, insistent gaze that everyone shake his hand and look him in the eye. The teacher was the last one in the room, by which time the students were at their desks with their books open, ready to begin.

During English class, Javhon, a wiry fourth-grade boy, volunteered to read his poem. When he spoke he had his finger in his mouth, and the teacher looked at him quizzically. "My tooth is falling out, but I want to read!" Javhon explained. After he finished reciting his poem, the teacher said, "Let's show Javhon some love for how much grit he showed! Now, go fix your tooth!" Before he dashed out of the room, the students acknowledged Javhon by snapping their fingers like they were at a poetry slam. The lesson wrapped up with the entire class chanting with a uniform beat as they stretched their arms to the sky: "We are scholars / on a mission / to shape our future. I matter! My education matters! My future matters! One hundred percent of the time!" After the chant died down, the teacher praised the class for their level of engagement, integrity, and respect. "I'm so proud of all of you. Look how many stars you've earned. [Indicating the wall chart] You are on your way—to college!"

Nothing is inherently wrong with these accolades; students should be praised, especially for effort. In addition, internalizing such terms such as "engagement" and "grit" may allow students to develop a more meta-cognitive approach, and learning how to reflect on and think about one's own learning can be very beneficial.

Yet I remain skeptical. Even though I appreciate the order and discipline demonstrated in hallways and classrooms, everyone was in lock-step. Each classroom felt the same, and teachers were all trained to teach and speak about respect, grit, teamwork, integrity, and engagement in similar ways. Consistent discipline is critical for a healthy school culture, but when I entered another classroom, I saw the downside of stressing routines and behavior above all else, including learning.

Twenty-five third graders sat crossed-legged on the rug facing their teacher and a big video screen. "As you know, we are about to begin our snake unit, and this is the video I promised yesterday that we would watch." A hand shot up. A little girl with many braids and ribbons in her hair asked in an awed whisper, "Is this the one where we get to see the snake actually walk out of its skin?" "Yes, we will see that, and we will take notes like scientists as we watch, and make some sketches." Everyone nodded eagerly. The teacher distributed clipboards and paper and pencils. A nervous excitement rippled through the class. Clearly, this was a lesson that they had been eagerly anticipating. "When we are all ready, like Amanda and Juan, sitting up and tracking me, I'll turn on the video." The students repositioned themselves and held their clipboards at the ready in their laps. However, two students in the back row of the rug were overtaken with giggles and seemed to have a hard time either putting in the paper or paying attention. The teacher redirected them a couple of times, but they were clearly in a world of their own. All others had their eyes facing forward and weren't paying much attention to the two gigglers. But suddenly, the teacher said, "It's clear to me that the class is not ready to engage in learning. Let's go back to our desks until we have one hundred percent engagement. You are not respecting the learning process. You have forgotten completely about SLANT-ing. Did you lose your back muscles over the weekend? Too many of you are slouching. I am going to begin to hand out demerits." The little girl with the braids whispered to her friend, "We aren't showing respect." Her friend nodded gravely. The students quietly got to their feet and, with an air of despondence, trooped silently back to their desks. "Now we will have to wait until tomorrow to see the video," the little girl said sadly, "and I really don't want a demerit."

When the class was dismissed for lunch, the teacher demanded that everyone line up silently. As they proceeded to the cafeteria, they passed a second-grade class who were walking in "hugs and bubbles" formation. These eight-year-olds held their arms crisscrossed across their chests almost like they were in a straitjacket. Their cheeks were puffed out as if they had caught a bubble inside. They too proceeded silently to the cafeteria, where they finally dropped their arms and relaxed their expressions. There were five different classes in the cafeteria, and all of them ate in complete silence while teachers monitored the room. I inquired if this silent lunch was punishment for bad behavior and was informed that silent lunch was a regular occurrence. "We want students to be able to have some time in the day where they are quiet and peaceful." But it felt anything but peaceful to me. It seemed more like a prison, with the teachers as guards. I was stunned that this had become a regular practice. Gone is the joy of meeting friends at lunch and chattering about anything or nothing. Gone is just being a carefree kid. None of the students in this school are white. As in many schools, almost all of the teachers are young and white. What message does this send to kids who are not of the dominant culture? This school felt oppressive to me.

While making eye contact or tracking or nodding at speakers is not wrong, this SLANT system isn't contextualized to a variety of learning environments. Its use in this school results in an emphasis on behavior over active learning. In other words, you are considered a good learner if you can demonstrate SLANT, but this is a minimal condition for learning in most situations. For many students, this behavior has nothing at all to do with learning. Of course it's hard to teach if two students are cutting up in class, but the third-grade science teacher described above had clearly been trained to stop the lesson in the absence of 100 percent compliance. In our conversation later, the teacher admitted to me that she felt bad about her decision to abort the lesson to focus on behavior. "In this school we believe that if students aren't practicing the behaviors we teach [SLANT], then learning will be compromised. It's like the broken windows theory. You have to take care of the small things before you take on the big things or nothing will get fixed."

A colleague of mine from the Boston Public Schools invited me to visit her "no excuses" school. I was curious as to why she had left a ten-year career teaching middle school in a more financially secure school district for a charter school. "Here I can teach. There are no behavior issues. And if there are, the dean immediately deals with them. All teachers have the same expectations for kids and use the same behavior systems. Kids start out with ninety points on Monday and if they don't get lower than seventy by Friday, they get to have a fun activity." She then showed me the "Merit/Demerit/Automatic Detention Tracking Sheet." There were eighty-three items listed: twenty-nine were for merits such as genuine enthusiasm, excellent posture, volunteering, urgency, and caring/kindness, and the remaining fifty-four were for demerits such as talking out of turn, poor attitude, grooming, and being off-task. Some of the latter were classified as automatic detentions, such as "jaywalking," "severe lack of urgency," or "profanity."

I was curious about "jaywalking" until I visited classrooms. Each classroom had a big red arrow in between rows of desks that pointed toward the whiteboard at the front of the room, and a big red arrow pointing down from the board toward the entrance. These arrows indicated the directions students should walk in the classroom. All classrooms in this school were set up identically, with three rows of eight to ten desks in pairs, with two students sitting together called "shoulder partners." There were twenty-eight students in each room, and all classrooms implemented a clear code of behavior that involved responding to commands from the teacher about when to sit, stand, clap, snap, or turn and talk to one's shoulder partner. SLANT was also employed in this school, and students who were out of line in any number of ways wore a different color T-shirt over their uniform and could not work with their shoulder partner. They were in the classroom but had to work in isolation. At the end of one class I observed, the teacher reminded students where they had excelled on the behavioral chart of merit/demerit expectations. Pointing to the chart, she said, "You were engaged in class, but you were not professional. You struggled with urgency and filing and getting to your seats on time. Now, sit up straight to get ready for your next class!" Then the teacher called out, "Thank you!" and students re-sponded, "Thank you!" The next class began.

I actually thought I had just watched a scene in a play. I couldn't be-lieve it was real. The values of submission, obedience, and self-control overshadowed any other possible values, except for grit. Students in this school have some of the highest standardized test scores in the state, and teachers praise the grittiness of their students, but I was frankly stunned by the rigidity of the behavior protocols. Again, most of the students (over 95 percent) are students of color, and I saw no teachers of color in this school. My colleague assured me that students were all happy and that teacher turnover was low. "I'm telling you, this works. I can teach here." Having been a middle school teacher, I can certainly appreciate the need for clarity about expectations and behavior, but this rigidity seems excessive. As educator Joan Goodman points out, "You can't re-ally do this kind of instruction if you don't have very submissive chil-dren who are capable of high levels of inhibition and do whatever they're told."[13] This kind of structure seems to assume that students start with bad behavior and that only through strictly adhering to a rigid discipline policy will students learn.

I understand and agree with the importance of a calm classroom, but the mechanistic and even slavish adherence to SLANT that I have wit-nessed in many no-excuses schools makes me wonder about the message we are sending to young people. Of course, clear discipline and behavioral expectations have a lot of benefit. But the word that kept coming to mind was "oppressive." Little room existed for divergent thinking. I reflected on another school I visited which was the opposite of a no-excuses school.

In an urban public school in New York City I witnessed a group of thirty eighth graders discussing the novel *If Beale Street Could Talk*, by James Baldwin. What struck me, in addition to their professional level of discourse, was how they had arranged themselves in the classroom. Some sat on top of their desks; others were on chairs and a few were standing. Not everyone was in a circle. One young man sat outside the circle and participated in the discussion even though he looked angry the entire time. Another student sat at the teacher's desk.

When I asked the teacher, Mr. Johnson, if their seating arrangement was distracting to him or to other students, he looked at me curiously.

"Why should it matter how they sit if they are participating and respecting one another's opinions? That's my goal. Can they talk to one another from the text, can they find evidence about their points of view, can they build off of what each other says?" But what about the fact that not everyone was living by the same rules? Clearly, the directions were to sit in a circle. "Look," he began somewhat impatiently with me, "Would I like everyone in a circle? Of course! Do I want to sacrifice valuable teaching and learning time to be constantly reminding students of those expectations? And more importantly, do I want to make sure that the classroom is a place where there is also some breathing room? I know what's going on with Carlos and Edward. I know why they have moved out of the circle. The rest of the class doesn't care."

I wasn't sure I was satisfied with his answers. I wanted to know if Mr. Johnson had seen the practices in many no-excuses schools where rules were easily and quickly adhered to, and teachers then felt that teaching could begin. "Of course," he told me. "Many of these students have come from schools like that—or they were asked to leave those schools because they weren't 'disciplined' enough [he held up his fingers to make quotation marks]. Carlos is still smarting from the memory of his last school. And, by the way, you won't see those ubiquitous college banners all over my walls. My job is to teach my students to think, and I know this may sound political, but to get them to think for themselves!" I agree with that goal, yet I was uncomfortable with the lack of structure or consequences for behavior in his classroom. I wondered if some of the no-excuses pedagogy would be of use in this case. Couldn't this teacher see how well behaved the students were in those schools, and wasn't he impressed by their test scores? Clearly, they also had learned to listen to one another. He countered, "I know that many of my colleagues believe that by following that formula of SLANT and no-excuses kind of practices, kids will get to college in large numbers and get out of the 'ghetto' [again, his quotes], but I don't think they are asking the students, or the community that the students come from, what success would look like for them. I think what's missing here is learning about self-determination and advocacy for oppressed peoples everywhere. I know it's a lot to ask of teachers, but we cannot keep seeing ourselves as ahistorical beings. We, as teachers, and particularly white teachers like me, need to understand that students of color are in this situation because of systemic racism. We have to all critically examine how we might be perpetuating that." Mr. Johnson went on to describe how his students were doing in high school. "The ones that challenge me the most are often the students who do the best in high school and then college. They know how to think critically *and independently.*"

The bottom line is this: are KIPP's (and, by extension, other "no-excuses" school models') methods effective? The intent was clear in all of the classrooms and schools I visited: by demonstrating aspects of TIGER, or whatever variant (teamwork, integrity, grit, engagement, and respect), everyone would learn together and everyone could go to college. However, the data is not in yet. Yes, there were early positive returns. According to a study commissioned by KIPP, "The vast majority of KIPP middle schools produced positive and statistically significant impacts on student achievement. Students from these schools showed gains in reading and math in all four years after they entered KIPP. . . . Three years after entering KIPP schools, many students experience achievement gains that are approximately equivalent to an additional year of instruction—enough to substantially narrow race- and income-based achievement gaps."[14] KIPP schools, by and large, showed significant gains on state tests, often outranking their district counterparts. They did this by spending more money per pupil than their home districts, through intensive tutoring, a longer school day, and an adherence to rigid behavioral practices. However, what we don't know is whether their elementary students will do well in college, where following directions is not necessarily the most valued skill. There seems to be little research on charter students' college achievement, but KIPP is one of the few charter management organizations (CMOs) that has allowed outside researchers to study their methods and results. One result I can cite is that in 2008, when BAA college graduation rates hovered around 64 percent, KIPP rates were only about 35 percent.[15]

KIPP is hoping to see great success from helping their students internalize grit. They may prove what psychologists like Duckworth hope: the more grit you have, the better you will do in the end. As often happens in education, however, we may have just latched on to the next new thing. The benefits of grit and lockstep learning may have been overinterpreted, and traits such as curiosity and creativity given short shrift. The boys who giggle the most may actually be the most curious learners later on. Those twenty-first-century competencies of critical thinking, collaboration, communication, and creativity that employers and others insist are the key to a productive and competitive economy are not well served by the no-excuses approach. However, when we can connect grit to what we now call a *growth mindset*, perhaps more significant learning for young people can occur.

MORE THAN GRIT: A GROWTH MINDSET

In *Mindset: The New Psychology of Success*, Carol Dweck describes two different mindsets. The first she calls a "fixed mindset," a belief that intelligence is static. Although you can learn new things, you can't change how intelligent you are. You are either smart or not smart. People with fixed mindsets don't believe that effort can change intelligence and so they have a very deterministic view of the world. "I'm not a good reader no matter how much I try." Or, "Math is always hard for me. I'll never be good at it." In contrast, an individual with a "growth mindset" believes that she can always increase her intelligence. Someone with a growth mindset sees "effort as the path to mastery" and is willing to learn through criticism and persist in the face of challenges.

I've had so many students who tell me: "I can't do this. I'm just not smart enough." Yet Dweck's ideas helped in our teaching of such students who could, in fact, develop a growth mindset. Along the way, we created some important connections between grit and growth. When grit is discussed within the context of a growth mindset, it is less of a stand-alone pedagogy. Also, we recognized, as did Duckworth, that grit is not just about perseverance over time, but also passion over time. Since BAA is ever focused on student passion, we wanted to better understand these connections. Dweck's work complemented our observations about our students.

The BAA faculty committed to read the book and discuss how to adapt our teaching to embrace this new psychology of success. We had talked and shared for years our frustrations about how our students seemed to be able to successfully run a sprint in mastering content and skills for a score on a test. Yet, to successfully run a marathon required different muscle conditioning and development. Our students were great performers in the moment, but needed to develop the persistence and dedication of marathon runners. We have teachers and staff who run annually in the famous Boston Marathon. To complete a marathon, they train over time and believe they can accomplish something incredibly difficult—even when they doubt their ability. We wanted our students to adopt *that* kind of mindset.

Dweck possessed insights we could use. We began by increasing the commitment to our summer reading program. In this program students worked in small groups over a five-week period and improved reading scores by two grade levels. Our curriculum reflected an understanding of growth mindset and we began to realize the power of developing lessons that helped students see themselves as powerful and competent readers. We also structured classes so that students would feel stretched by their reading levels but not overwhelmed. We began to explore the literature about how to help students increase their independent reading skills and how to be more purposeful as teachers about determining those levels. We wanted everyone to see themselves as readers and writers with muscles that could expand.

In response to Dweck's work and our literacy explorations, one of BAA's veteran teachers created something called the "reading zone" in which the idea of just relaxing and reading a book in her classroom was expected and honored. While in class, students would be guided through difficult reading passages, but in the reading zone the idea was to engage one's own curiosity and passions. I loved visiting her class while the reading zone was in session. I had never seen high school kids sprawled on the floor so engaged in *their* book of choice. I could almost feel muscles flexing. Even the most reluctant readers began to talk about themselves as readers and writers. "I never really read a whole book. I just read what was assigned for a class," said one student. "I didn't think I was smart enough to read a whole book." Dweck would have been pleased.

These academic studies of grit and growth mindset intrigued me, and many of my faculty. Our discussions of "sprint versus marathon" were our way of talking about grit, about goal setting, about stick-to-it-ness, of learning to believe in oneself. Yet we took care not to do it in a vacuum that didn't include close analysis of issues of access and equity. We discussed how to help students "strengthen their core" in order to deal with problems or issues that continued to knock them off center. These included ESL issues or caring for a younger sibling or even coming from a neighborhood plagued with poverty. When anything interfered with a student's studies or abilities to succeed, we took responsibility to help them reassess. That's where the notion of a strong core comes in. Having this language earlier in my career would have helped me to better guide Rosa. Nevertheless, we must be clear with students that access and equity are *not* individually determined. We must teach our students that, no matter how strong their core is, structures still exist that subordinate some learners, particularly if they are poor and not white. A lot more grit and strength are needed to succeed in college if you are poor or a person of color than if you are white and middle class.

"Work hard and you will be successful" is a deeply imbedded belief in our society. It undergirds the America dream and supports a belief that this country is a meritocracy. In fact, much of this "new" psychology supports the dream: if you show grit and persistence and embrace a growth mindset, you will access opportunity and success. Still, enormous dangers lurk in how these experiments and theories have been interpreted in classrooms and schools. Without intense interrogation we might assume that success is individually created and sustained. "If I could do it, so can you" is how so much of this "grit" work gets translated into practice. The assumption of how you can "pull yourself up by your bootstraps" becomes nearly impossible to break. The no-excuses world of schools seems to ignore reams of data that repeatedly show how poverty, social class, race, and parents' educational attainment more directly influence an individual's success and potential earnings than any individual effort. Individual effort is still vitally important, but a student's circumstances still do impact his or her future, and we can't ignore these additional important factors.

As we at BAA discussed with students and among ourselves the work of Dweck, Duckworth, Tough, and others, we were intrigued by other character traits in the literature such as zest, curiosity, and optimism. We were particularly captivated by *optimism,* since this seemed elusive for many of our students. Optimism, according to the research, doesn't necessarily mean *happy*; rather it denotes a belief in one's own agency.[16]

Or, to use one of Dweck's terms again: a belief in one's growth mindset. Noam Chomsky has said, "Optimism is a strategy for making a better future. Because unless you believe that the future can be better, you are unlikely to step up and take responsibility for making it so."[17] This definition framed much of what we wanted to teach our students.

In art making, optimism, or the confidence that you can make work, is key to actually producing it. Otherwise, you are frozen in front of your blank page. When faced with an artistic medium, whether a visual one such as paint or clay or a kinesthetic one such as dance, you must first believe that you *can and deserve* to make work. You need a modicum of certainty that your ideas matter. We discussed the ways in which making art gave many of our most learning-challenged, or special-needs students, another lens or insight into themselves and their own worth. Miguel is an example. He was severely dyslexic, had ADHD, and did poorly in academic subjects. As he began to emerge as a skilled actor and designer, his ability to pay attention and work through his reading struggles became less fraught and emotional. He knew he had enormous strengths in other areas. We knew that in the arts our students were continually exposed to dispositions or traits like optimism. We actually called them skills or habits of mind.

Curiosity is another trait that may be as important if not more important than grit. In my experience, curiosity is related to creativity, imagination, and exploration—which our students also deserve the time and space to cultivate. This need not be just a phenomenon for arts classes. Examples such as the reading zone can support students' curiosity through both guided inquiry and leisure reading. Science classes can lend themselves to discovery and invention and opportunities to create and test hypotheses about many different scenarios. Our current obsession with grit begins to obliterate the ability to wonder—or relegate it only to the upper classes.

Our experience teaching the arts required us to include long periods of thinking through problems in both academic and arts classrooms. Mary Helen Immordino-Yang writes convincingly that "rest is not idleness."[18] Engagement may look very different depending on the student and the kind of problem she is trying to solve or express. To persuasively present a monologue requires deep thinking about that character. To an outsider, a student lying on the floor lost in a character study or visualizing how to build the tallest tower from Dixie cups might seem to be doing nothing, when in fact the mind's gears are steadily turning. I couldn't imagine that a typical no-excuses classroom would ever allow the circumstances for such rumination.

EVIDENCE OF INEQUALITY

Context matters. One 2014 study followed 790 students from twenty Baltimore public elementary schools over three decades.[19] The results are extremely disturbing in terms of educational and socioeconomic outcomes.[20] While many disadvantages, such as lack of educational attainment, drug involvement, and prison convictions, were similar for whites and blacks, in the study, "white privilege" accounted for dramatically higher-paying jobs for white men in the trades than for black men (50 percent to 15 percent, respectively). Through various family and community connections, whites had greater access to unions than blacks. Furthermore, despite similar stressors with drugs, the law more adversely affected blacks than whites in terms of higher percentage of incarceration and more difficulties of entry into the work force. As the authors point out, if we refuse to confront the "long shadow" of racism, which they document carefully in this study, we are doing our youth a disservice. If these students had been more exposed to "grit" as the dominant instructional pedagogy, outcomes may well have been improved for some, but achievement is far more complicated than a new psychology or technique. If we ignore race, poverty, and social class we continue to create false promises for too many young people. It is this tension that I want educators to embrace and not set up false dichotomies about how rigid behavioral expectations can be the cure-all to systemic oppression. In fact, I want us to interrogate how these systems of behavioral management may be doing more to institutionalize racist expectations of young people.

THE STORIES: BAA GRADUATES WORK HARD

BAA practiced a very different way of teaching grit. Certainly in an arts school, embracing challenges, persisting in the face of difficulty, and seeing effort as the path toward mastery are all key components of the student experience. Artists learn from criticism, called "critique" in the visual arts or "juries" in music or theater. Our curriculum requires students to deeply understand and find inspiration in the work of others, also part of Dweck's description of a growth mindset. The idea that intelligence is not static and can be developed seemed both obvious and revolutionary to us. It was deeply embedded in our arts curriculum as well as the pedagogy of our academic teachers.

An explicit and implicit expectation existed at BAA that if students worked hard, they would be successful. "At least that's what you guys always said," Clara, a BAA alumna, remarked in our discussion. I explicitly said similar things to students, and I believed it. Even though I had failed with Rosa, I still had to believe that hard work would gain my students entry into a society that marginalized them. They would be living proof that individuals could make it. They would break those glass ceilings. They would prove all the naysayers wrong. But as I listened to my alumni interviewees, a range of viewpoints surfaced. In this section, the stories told by three different graduates highlight that working hard and doing everything right does not automatically equal success. Through their reflections, I came to more deeply understand the ways in which their achievements were fashioned, and to better understand my own assumptions about how we reach and recognize success in high schools. All three are on the road to success, but none of their journeys has been straightforward or easy. The injustices that they experienced and their difficulties in navigating life after high school made me wonder if I had done enough to prepare them. Had I been naïve in some way? In my insistence that their hard work would allow them to achieve success I had underestimated the negative and pervasive effects of race, social class, and also immigrant status throughout the educational pipeline. Reviewing my conversations with Clara, I kept returning to possible instances where I might have interceded differently. In Ty's situation we see the advantages of more middle-class experiences and the role of family experience. As I listened to Ali, I was struck by how we prepared her to face obstacles, learn to be flexible, and not give up. The ways in which our graduates interpreted growth mindset, grit, or optimism served them well on most occasions; nevertheless their experiences provided insight into the failures of the systems we have yet to dismantle.

CLARA'S STORY: FAR MORE THAN GRIT

Clara was always quick to volunteer to be an ambassador for BAA and enjoyed showing visitors the high school, of which she was immensely proud. She was bilingual (Spanish and English) and could talk as easily to Latino families as she could to potential funders. She had a gentle ease and graciousness about her and a gift for making others feel comfortable. At Senior Awards Night, Clara was honored for her commitment to service, her peers, and her school. And yet she has languished in college, having saved enough money after three years of working full-time to take only one course a semester. She expressed regret, and even anger, over the gap between who she was in high school and what she is dealing with now.

Clara was considered a role model because of the way she embodied BAA's "habits of the graduate" or RICO: refining, inventing, connecting, and owning their work. The learning processes that RICO represented fascinated Clara, and she could easily articulate how her teachers engaged her and others artistically and academically. "Artists are never satisfied. They are always refining their craft," she said. "That's what makes their work so powerful. You can't ever say, 'I'm done. This is perfect.' It's always in process." Clara felt that this orientation helped push her and her classmates to succeed at high levels and acknowledged how this mindset would help her tackle college work. "I see how so many of my friends are just memorizing stuff. Yeah, they may know more facts then me, but do they know to 'learn to learn'?" She understood that the process of learning was as important as the accumulation of knowledge or facts.

And yet, she also struggled academically—especially with her written work, which required many revisions. Clara is a second-language learner and comes from a very hard-working family. Her mother cleaned houses. Her little brother was doing all right in school, but needed a lot of attention. Her older brother had been deported. Although her mother had only a sixth-grade education, she was supportive of Clara's dreams and ambitions. Clara always thought that college would be in her future. When I asked her mother about her hopes for her daughter, she looked at her daughter almost shyly and said, in Spanish, "Whatever she dreams, she can do. I have watched her. I am so proud. She has worked so hard." She patted her daughter's hand and smiled. I did too.

When her best friend, Marilu, got into college with a full scholarship, Clara celebrated with her. "I just knew she'd get money. Who wouldn't want Marilu?! She so deserves this." She spoke without any jealousy. She was confident that her own scholarship and acceptance letter would follow.

But after a few weeks of hearing nothing, Clara came to me. "I think I have to become an emancipated minor." I looked at her quizzically. "My mother never filled out the financial aid forms. I didn't understand that she couldn't share her income information since my mom is undocumented." Clara thought she could become an emancipated minor and then apply on her own, but I knew it was too late in the year. We talked about going to community college and taking one course at a time so that she could work and pay out of pocket. Clara's eyes clouded. "That's not the way it's supposed to happen. I've done everything right here. I've worked hard."

Clara was right. She *had* worked hard. She had done everything right. But that didn't translate into college admissions with financial aid. Clara tried to maintain her focus for the next few weeks. And she was ecstatic at graduation with her family cheering her on—the first to graduate from high school. But when I tried to reach out to Clara after graduation to make sure that everything was set for community college, she didn't return my calls or text messages.

Finally, in the fall, I was able to talk with her. I wanted to know how things had spun so out of control. Why did she find out so late about her mother? Not until Clara realized that no acceptance letters were waiting for her did she confront her mother. "I knew she didn't have papers. But I didn't know that meant I couldn't get financial aid. No one talked to me about that. In some ways, 'cause I was always doing everything for everyone, I think teachers and my advisor just assumed I had all the college stuff together." Clara's mom had been involved in her daughter's education. She'd come to all the family conferences. I considered myself especially close to Clara, and I even knew about her brother being deported. But that had been years ago. I assumed that her mom had somehow acquired papers. Whenever I talked about Clara's mom filling out the financial aid papers, her mom agreed that she would. I believe she meant to. I believe she thought she could and didn't understand that obstacle in her legal status. We all were so impressed with Clara's determination to go to college that we had not drilled down deeper.

That fall, an anger and hardness edged her usually bright voice. "When I realized what had happened, I still thought I could go to community college, like you said, and just pay for one class, but I didn't even have that money. And I think I was so upset to realize that I couldn't get loans or financial aid if my mom couldn't share her information." It was as if everything she had worked for had just come crashing down on Clara. She talked about working at a sub shop. "As many hours as I can. My little brother's gotten sick, and I have to help my mother with the bills and everything." I had sent Clara a video of one of the presentations she had done about RICO. I wondered if she had enjoyed watching it. "Yeah, I got the video. But I haven't had time to watch it. I'm working all the time." I could feel the pain in her voice. She was worried that her best years were already behind her. And I felt that I had betrayed her. How had I not been perceptive enough or pushy enough to figure out what was going on with her family? To snip the invisible threads of inequity, there is always one more question that must be asked, one more piece of information that must be secured. The playing field is massively uneven; even if someone like Clara plays by the rules and does all the right things, success is not guaranteed.

A year later, Clara called me. She sounded so happy. "Guess what?" she asked brightly. "I just got one B and an A in my first semester in college!" "You're enrolled?" I practically screamed through the phone lines. "Of course I am, Nathan; what did you expect?" I grinned at Clara's habit of calling me (and all other BAA teachers) just by the last name. "I got promoted to manager and so I got paid more, and I just kept saving up. I think I can take two courses a semester. Yeah, it'll take me awhile, but it's worth it. You didn't think after all I did at BAA that I'd just quit studying?" Clearly, her "grit" had shown through—along with the kind of optimism that Noam Chomsky described, which allowed her to believe that she could write her own story, not accept one that could so easily have been written for her.

ALI'S STORY: ADAPTING AND PERSISTING

"You guys told me college would be hard, but I didn't understand that until I got there. Maybe no one does. You have to be *in* it to get it." The difference between being an honor's student in high school and a college student came as something of a shock to Ali. "You *did* tell us that no one would hold our hands, but it's another thing when you are actually experiencing it firsthand." Still, Ali had established a good work ethic in high school, and more importantly, she knew what support looked like. "The first thing I did when I got there was to find the Learning Center, and boy, did I need it. First semester I got a warning notice. Me? Honor roll student!"

As a theater student in high school, Ali always had an ensemble to talk with and a place to get perspective on her struggles. "I was from a single-parent home. My mom worked a ton, but she never really could get out of struggling to live paycheck to paycheck. I worked since I was able to help. Life wasn't easy, but I didn't know anything different. Until BAA." Ali said that being with peers who experienced issues such as parents in jail or on drugs or violence in the home or in the neighborhood taught her that all her classmates had their own difficulties.

One acting class in particular made a huge impression on Ali. The teacher was an industry professional and spoke honestly about how hard students should be prepared to work. "It was scary to hear her truth—about how she had worked as a server in a restaurant in order to pay her bills," Ali said, "but she was determined to break into the industry. She did, eventually, but she was poor for a long time." Ali shares how that class, and that teacher, "made me realize that if you wanted something badly enough, you really have to work for it. I decided I would get a four-year scholarship to college. I knew my mom couldn't pay for it. I had to go if I was ever going to really be someone." And her mom told her the same thing. Again and again.

In her tight-knit ensemble, everyone talked about his or her future goals, and Ali knew they all "would support each other to reach our dreams." Everyone was sure that Ali would go to college and get a degree to become a veterinarian. Every weekend when she wasn't in rehearsals, she worked in a vet's office. She knew more about dogs and cats than anyone in high school. Her friends always gave her Hello Kitty paraphernalia, and whenever there was a "code gray" in school—a mouse alert—the joke was that Ali would be sent to rescue the creature before it succumbed to a mousetrap. She was a staunch vegetarian, believing that "fish are friends, not food." She dreamed of having her own clinic and bringing health and happiness to animals and their owners.

"I was so excited to start college. I was proud that I got a four-year scholarship. I had already declared my major: biology, since I was going to be a vet. I knew I would do fine. Just like high school." But Ali didn't feel prepared for a huge lecture class whose main purpose was to weed people out. "I kept going to the professor—I knew about office hours and getting help—and I'd see my TA all the time. I was determined to pass that class, but I just kept sinking deeper and deeper. I was barely passing. I was so angry 'cause I knew that this class was important. I'd never failed anything. I wasn't going to fail."

Ali scraped by with a D. She started to meet with an academic coach from the Learning Center and continued through all four years of college. "She really helped me separate the details from the big picture of classes. I was drowning in the details. I guess that's what happened to me in biology. I kept trying to memorize the little things, but I never saw the big concepts and so things didn't make sense like they should have." The next semester Ali tried another big lecture class and managed to get a C-. She was distraught. Her academic advisor suggested that she change her major to psychology. "It was the biggest blow I'd ever received. No one ever told me I couldn't do something. And I know that's not what my advisor was really saying. But it felt that way. She tried to get me to see that there were lots of different ways to work with animals, other careers than being a vet. We talked about everything, including programs that trained graduates to work with penguins or dolphins. She even helped me get an internship at a dolphin center over the summer. It was amazing." Ali's world opened up, and she began to see so many different possibilities for herself. Maybe instead of being a vet she would pursue a career in research. She found herself fascinated by animal behavior and began to explore other classes and internships. "I had to remember my theater training. Sometimes in rehearsal when it's just not working and you just keep repeating the same objective, you need to hear the director or your scene partner say, 'Let's try it differently. Let's play with a new idea.' Then, suddenly, the connections happen and you're on fire. I had to let that happen for me in college, but it was harder. I felt like I was disappointing everyone from BAA who had always believed in me and my goals. And I was disappointing myself."

Ali switched her major and turned things around. She started working in the Learning Center to help other students like herself, and she began to think about all the possibilities she could pursue with a degree in psychology. "I even got a job at the Museum of Science, working with the animal trainers, and I was the one handling the snakes for the children's shows. It was just a thrill!" Ali met with tutors, her academic coach, and her professors whenever she could. She kept her grades up and got excited about behavioral psychology and lab work. "But I had another kind of freakout the spring semester of my junior year. I knew I had a full-time job waiting for me at the museum when I graduated, if I wanted it. Yet I had done a spring break service trip and had worked with a whale trainer. I just knew I wanted to be a marine biologist, but I didn't have the course requirements. I wanted to work with whales, dolphins, or penguins, but I knew how competitive those jobs were. I felt like a failure all over again. Yeah, holding snakes was cool, but it wasn't the same." Ali began to research how to become a trainer. She knew she had to take a diving course and get certified, but that cost a lot of money and would have to wait until after graduation. Ali graduated with honors with a degree in psychology and saved enough money to get certified. She continues to work at the museum with ambitions to be a sea mammal trainer, and is confident that within the next few years she will get her dream job. "It's the big picture that keeps me happy and moving forward. You have to have those dreams, but you have to be flexible enough to take a different approach. That's what BAA taught me and I'm very grateful." For now, she contents herself with visits to "her seals" at the aquarium or trips to Florida to visit Sea World. "I'll be one of those trainers one day. I know it."

Ali demonstrates grit and optimism, as well as enormous flexibility. Her hard work has paid off. She has a college degree and a good job.

Her mom is stable. She is headed where she wants to be, and she is living proof of why we adhere to the assumption that working hard ultimately leads to success.

TY'S STORY: FAMILY TIES THAT BIND

Like Ali, Ty transferred many of the skills he'd gained in high school to overcome great obstacles and graduate from engineering school in four years. This belief about overcoming amid adversity serves many students well as they aspire to be the next one to beat the odds. But for every Ty who manages to forge a traditional path to success, there are at least two Claras, who are forced onto detours they have to work twice as hard to find their way back from. The notion that "with grit everyone can make it" absolves us of the responsibility to look at political or racial or socioeconomic systems that work against students like Clara, whose parents' immigration status holds back their high-achieving children (one of the reasons so many families had hoped for passage of the DREAM Act).

Unlike Clara's mother, Ty's had finished high school and completed two years of college. Ty also had an uncle who was in the military in a fairly high position. An expectation existed that Ty would go to a four-year college, as would his younger brother and sister. Those were the family rules. More than once his mother said, "Ty will be the first. He will blaze the trail for his siblings. He knows that. He better not try to squeak by. He's going to college." Ty excelled at BAA. He loved math, science, and engineering, and he was also a skilled musician. He was on honor roll all four years and also distinguished himself as an ambassador for the school, much like Clara. At family conferences, his mother often brought the two younger children and made sure that they listened while she spoke to her son and his advisor. Ty's mom said, "We know too many folks—especially black folks—whose children are in jail or who haven't finished even high school. That's not Ty. He knows that. He's not going to be another negative statistic. Uh-uh." Ty's mom was always firm and clear. And so was Ty. Speaking with Clara, he once referred to himself as a "rare species." "You know people actually say that," Ty said. "Black males who go to college. There are so few of us." Clara laughed. In many respects, Ty's mom is a positive version of the "no excuses" model. She doesn't ignore cultural context, and she is clear about the role of family and friends. In her own way, she ensures that her son understands how to cross over into the dominant culture.

When Ty got to college, on a full scholarship, he started as an electrical engineering major, yet quickly struggled to keep up with his classes. "I was afraid I'd lose my scholarship. When I dipped to a 2.1 [GPA] after that first semester, I decided to switch majors. But first I called my mom. I knew she'd be furious, but I wanted her to understand that if I went as low as a 2.0, I'd lose the scholarship altogether. Mechanical engineering had a few less requirements." Ty's mom took a lot of convincing. She admitted to not really understanding the difference between electrical and mechanical engineering. She just didn't want her son to take the easy way out. But she didn't want him to lose his scholarship either. In the end, she agreed with her son's decisions.

Ty recounts how everyone struggled that first year, yet kids of color seemed to struggle the most. Ty got a D in chemistry, and he was also failing his math course that second semester. He worried about how he would tell his mother. "She just wouldn't understand how I could be failing, and after switching majors. I got more worried about that than anything else." Then, Ty found out that his roommate had switched into an online math course, so he did the same. "It was such a relief because it was on my own pace. I think I just wasn't prepared for the intensity of the work that first year. Other classmates at college seemed to come in with more math and science classes than I'd ever done." Ty appreciated his roommate's guidance, but still felt left out of some kind of secret society at college. How come he hadn't heard about the online math course? When he spoke to his advisor about it, the professor acted like it was no big deal: "Yes, go ahead and switch. Good idea." Ty wanted to press harder and find out where students found out about such opportunities and options, but he didn't know how to frame the question.

Ty didn't lose his scholarship that first year, and when he returned to campus as a sophomore, the first thing he did was to get a tutor. He remembered meeting people from the National Society of Black Engineers (NSBE) when they visited BAA and had recently seen a poster on campus advertising their tutoring services. "Once I signed up for that, I could breathe again. Suddenly I was with all the other black kids, and the Hispanic kids too." Ty hadn't realized how racially isolated he'd felt all freshman year. Everything had been coming at him so fast and furiously, and he'd just been trying to stay afloat. He hadn't taken the time to notice how lonely he felt, even with his participation in the Robotics Club filling in his social life a bit. "Class was usually a sea of white and Asian faces. I just wanted to pass and not lose my scholarship, but when I joined the NSBE, everything changed. That's where I met my best friends. That's really where I learned to study. That's where I felt at home. I hadn't realized how I constantly felt I was being judged as not as smart—like, inferior to everyone else." However, under the auspices of NSBE, he felt certain he could graduate and excel. "I am not sure why I had to take a whole year to learn about NSBE. I don't remember hearing about them at orientation. I guess the feeling was, you got here, you can make it." But Ty knew he needed more help. He didn't know how difficult it could be to figure out the rules of a game so new to him.

Finding the online math course was key to Ty's successful completion of his degree requirements, as was finding his "posse" in the National Society of Black Engineers. But Ty was lucky to have stumbled on these experiences—one, thanks to a roommate; the other, because he happened upon a poster. Yet our assumption is that he simply worked hard and found success. We could tell the story that way and it wouldn't be wrong. But it ignores the invisible threads of inequity that are far less likely to tighten around the necks of our dominant-culture students. Furthermore, Ty's success fuels the ways many schools embrace the role of "noncognitive" skills as a determinant of academic success. We could say that Ty had all the grit and conscientiousness and resiliency that we hope for in young people. Along with that, he had strong familial support for finishing college (as well as examples of professionals in his own family) and a lot of luck. There are so many students like Ty who work hard, show enormous determination and flexibility, and still don't make it.

GRIT IS NOT SUFFICIENT

The vocabulary popularized by writers like Paul Tough, Carol Dweck, and Angela Duckworth has become part of the popular myths or assumptions about why some young people succeed and others do not. When we understand better how their theories were developed and for what contexts, we can then examine their validity for schools and how to critically apply them to evolving classroom practices. None of these writers intended for their ideas to become the next fad in schools. We must be vigilant in our discussions so that we don't create "grit" or "growth mindset" schools devoid of deep understanding of cultural, racial, and social class contexts.

We want to allow for growth mindsets in a way that might equalize the playing field, yet we continue to entrap so many of our young people with the assumption that if they just play by the rules, do the right things, they will be successful. Achieving high test scores has become the only way to measure success or to prove that students have learned grit. Equating better test results with healthy learning has reduced many schools to a narrow understanding of learning. KIPP and other no-excuses organizations now acknowledge that deeper learning does not occur just by teaching behavioral techniques. Their early results, as measured by the improved test scores of their students, do not equate to higher high school or college graduation rates. Other no-excuses CMOs are also repudiating their earlier slavish dedication to grit-like practices. We may be entering into the end of the no-excuses era. I hope so.

EMBRACING BOTH:
CREATIVITY AND FLEXIBILITY

We have learned from the journeys of Clara, Ali, Ty, and Rosa, whose story highlights how having grit isn't sufficient as a K–12 student, especially if your teachers or "the system" don't recognize your potential or hear your self-advocacy. I believe that at BAA we taught our students to have a very strong "core." We did our best to teach them about how to navigate the world after high school into college. But was it enough? Clara would have needed superhuman grit to fully understand her mother's situation and how it was going to detrimentally affect her. However, she did adjust her entire life plan and she didn't give up. She continued to work hard. Ali certainly showed tremendous grit and persistence as she struggled to make her dreams come true. She demonstrated enormous flexibility as she turned from a study of biology to psychology while continuing to pursue her dream of working with animals and has been able to keep them and their behavior as a central part of her work life. Ty perhaps should have known earlier how to access help, but at least he didn't learn too late. Grit was clearly an important factor in Ty's success, but he also would not have succeeded had it not been for his family support and the resources that they provided.

When we talk about working hard, we might also talk about flexibility, which all of these students demonstrated. All three developed skills of resiliency. Yet again I am reminded of how an education immersed in arts and creativity teaches skills about making choices, using one's judgment, being flexible, and finding a new way to solve a problem. Learning the discipline of an art form, or any other discipline that connects perseverance with practice and passion, prepares a student to use those skills in other realms. Elliot Eisner writes, "The arts teach children that in complex forms of problem solving purposes are seldom fixed, but change with circumstance and opportunity. Learning in the arts requires the ability and a willingness to surrender to the unanticipated possibilities of the work as it unfolds."[21] Causality is always difficult to prove. Duckworth posited a connection between passion and perseverance and higher achievement. Perhaps she didn't go far enough and embrace the role that creativity—which need not be reserved for art students alone—might play.

BAA is exploring how to be a school that privileges a growth mindset while embracing creativity as a way to academic achievement. BAA also teaches that while it's important to work hard toward your goals, it's also critical to think about one's individual success within the context of community change. One project that brings together all these ideas is the Senior Grant process. Students begin this process in their junior year. For many, their first reaction to the assignment, which they understand will span two years, is, "This is too much work" or, "This is impossible." But through a carefully calibrated process, all students meet the goals of the assignment. By applying their artistic and academic skills, students create a project or program that responds to a community need. The projects are rooted in students' passions and bring enormous creativity to problem solving. For example, students have made films to help other young people better understand drug addiction. One student produced a one-woman show that uncovered the issue of homelessness in teens. Another produced a hip-hop concert to raise awareness about neighborhood violence. In each instance, students have to work within the constraints of a grant proposal (or letter of intent) while demonstrating their understanding of the complexities of the issue. They also demonstrate their presentation and writing skills by explaining both orally and in writing how their plans correspond to solutions and why they should be funded. While all students have to submit individual work and are judged separately, they can work together in teams. All of this is a learning process. Over the years, almost all students, funded or not, have found ways to incorporate their projects into future life plans.

We haven't renamed this Senior Grant Project as "Teaching Growth Mindset," but I think it's a reasonable example and could be adapted for any school. Students learn the importance of using their own grit, perseverance, hard work, and creativity for the greater good. The notion that a school, as an evolving institution, can and should serve its community is deeply embedded in the fabric of BAA. There can be a collective power for change when creativity is at the center of work.

While exploring some of the detrimental ways that I have seen grit imposed on students, I've become convinced that more educators should instead embrace the role of creativity in their teaching. I also conclude that more schools could incorporate capstone projects that encourage students to persist over time to solve complex problems. In our classrooms and schoolyards, we must encourage risk taking, learning from mistakes, and multiple ways to be flexible. I believe such an approach will serve students better than lockstep learning. Nevertheless, I have learned through listening to my students that we must not forget that our schools and communities exist within a racist society that is replete with systemic oppression. Breaking those barriers requires more than one individual's efforts. Our work as teachers, school leaders, and policy makers is not complete unless we continue to insist on change.

CHAPTER FOUR

"Everyone Can Go to College"

I have always believed that getting into and successfully graduating from college remain the most important goals of pre-K–12 education. Two generations of college-educated family members precede me. Growing up, I always knew I would be college-bound—as did my children. The notion that some kids just aren't college material troubled me and helped direct me into teaching. This label, "Not college material," is often imposed unfairly on those who are poor or have black or brown skin color. In this country, a college education is touted as the best preparation for life as a successful adult. I agree. My concern is the question of equity and how we can be satisfied with a society in which entire segments of the population lack access to a college degree. This lack of equity drove my passion to ensure that my students shared in the intellectual, cultural, and artistic development of the college experience, as well as the opportunities that a degree ensured—namely, access to a middle-class life. When I led BAA, I expected that all students would go to college and finish with a degree. I championed that narrative. *Everyone* was college material.

As I began researching this book, listening to and learning from my alumni, I started to question my own assumptions and convictions. Many former students talked about how they wished for more guidance about career preparation that might *not* require a college degree. Without using the actual words, they talked about their desire for more specific career and vocational education. "Do you need a college degree to be an auto mechanic, a carpenter, a stage hand?" students would ask. "How do you enter those jobs that have a union?" "Couldn't I make good money as a barber or a baker?" Others talked about how more permission and encouragement from teachers and administrators to work for a couple of years and then attend college might have allowed them to approach their education with a more mature outlook. These students needed to explore the world in a different way than I, as headmaster, espoused. I worried about kids taking time off to work for fear that they would lose the supportive network of advisors, guidance counselors, and teachers who helped them with applications. College deferment and "gap years" were really only options for students from families who didn't need to worry about money. Even though we always had a few faculty without degrees, most staff were college-educated. As a school, college attendance was a guiding principle, consistent with the understanding that a college education is almost a necessity to compete in our economy. The data about earnings are incontrovertible. Without some college, most young people will not be able to live a life that approaches middle-class standards. Kati Haycock, founder of the Education Trust, has written and spoken persuasively about a four-year college degree as the only sure route out of poverty. And yet, this chapter poses an uncomfortable question: Is college really the right course for everyone?

What if we expand the notion of postsecondary education? Could career and technical education *done well* provide a different road map for many students? What if educators began to discuss career readiness as a legitimate and respectable pathway? This chapter investigates how we might rethink the role of career and technical education as providing opportunity for young people. Must pre-K–12 education continue to be *either* about academics *or* career preparation?

Historically, vocational education has tracked poor and minority youth into nonacademic coursework that has led to lower high school graduation rates and fewer college opportunities. However, as career and technical education (CTE) has replaced vocational education, the popularity of these programs has grown across the country. (Right now, only one in twenty US public high schools is a full-time CTE school, and many of these schools have a waiting list.)[1] Researchers are also closely monitoring high school graduation rates of students enrolled in these programs.[2] In fact, a recent study of a program in California called Linked Learning Alliance suggests that high school students who have exposure to both college-prep and career and technical education courses have higher graduation rates.[3] In Linked Learning districts, students at all levels of achievement are enrolled in CTE courses, thus avoiding any tracking system. Those who take three or more courses in one career area have a higher high school graduation rate than students in the regular college-bound track. These findings were on my mind as I talked to many of my alums.

This chapter takes you on the journey that broadened my thinking. We meet a variety of young people who wished for different opportunities. I visit and discuss different CTE schools. Two hold enormous promise for CTE done well. The other raises concerns about the racial, structural, and historical impediments to high-quality CTE education. I also visited countries where apprenticeship programs are considered as prestigious as a college degree. I hope that what I learned challenges popular assumptions and helps us think deeply and differently about the purpose(s) of schooling.

EVERYONE CAN GO TO COLLEGE

The current national rhetoric insists that everyone can and should go to college. Many remember President Obama's first address to a joint session of Congress when he echoed the theme of college for all. "We will provide the support necessary for you to complete college and meet a new goal: by 2020, America will once again have the highest proportion of college graduates in the world."[4] A recent blog post on *College Parents of America* attempts to lessen parental anxiety about their children getting into college: "It sounds like a cliché but there really is a college for everyone."[5] The article reminds parents that while approximately 150 highly selective colleges hold a particular allure for families, there are almost 4,000 other US colleges and universities out there. These non-elite colleges generally accept over 50 percent of their applicants. So, the article concludes, "getting into, and performing well, in the vast majority of schools in the US is still pretty much a wide-open book, ready to be written by your sons and daughters, the current and future college students of America."[6] There it is. All of our high school graduates can and should go to college. Certainly in some places in this country, especially in urban centers where farming and manufacturing jobs are almost nonexistent, graduates without a college degree will be relegated, for the most part, to unskilled jobs.

However, disadvantaged youth in the United States remain largely without the support necessary to attend and then succeed in college. Though previous chapters have addressed the financial and systemic barriers to access and retention, this chapter considers whether "college for all" should continue to be the goal. Is college still the only avenue to a comfortable life?

Even with best efforts and a laser focus on college acceptance rates, some students will not enroll in college. As we've seen, of the 94 percent of BAA graduates accepted to college, only about two-thirds actually go. Drawing from data collected in 2012, we found that 65 percent of Boston Arts Academy students enrolled in college. For the same year, 52 percent of Boston Public School students (this figure includes the three exam schools where students passed an academic test for entrance) enrolled in college, and nationally, 52.5 percent of high school graduates enrolled. There is one other interesting enrollment statistic that is worthy of comparison: low-income enrollment in college. BAA excels in the enrollment of low-income students, and its 62.9 percent average is well above state (49.6 percent), national (52.5 percent), and city (48.3 percent) averages.[7]

Yet we can see that roughly a third of our high school graduates are not going to college. What are we doing to prepare those students for an alternative path to success? Or what *should* we be doing? College or poverty should not be their only choices. I staunchly believe we need more options—and career preparation may be an important avenue forward, giving our students more possibilities for both completing college and securing professional employment. A recent *New York Times* opinion piece stated, "more than 600,000 jobs remain open in the manufacturing sector. . . . These are jobs that provide a middle-class wage without a traditional four-year college degree."[8] These "middle-skilled" jobs, as they are often called, accounted for 54 percent of the nation's jobs in 2012, and the demand for these jobs continues to rise.[9] High schools should play a significant role in getting youth and young adults to experience work and the labor market.

Initial reaction to vocational or career educational approaches often continues to be, "That's for the working class, not for my students or children" or, "Vocational education is racially tracked and unjust." And it's true that these concerns should be continually raised, since an overemphasis on job-specific skills can lead to dividing students based on perceived abilities—or tracking. To put it more bluntly, are STEM career-training programs offered more often to white students and law enforcement opportunities provided more frequently to black and brown students? Schools and districts, which are embracing a renewed focus on career academies, must remain vigilant that career academies are not reinforcing age-old inequalities for students of color. Louis F. Rodriguez writes that all career academies must pay attention to enrollment patterns by race, language, and social class.[10] Most importantly, career academies need to offer academically rigorous coursework. Learning to apply academic skills and content to actual work situations is an essential part of deeper learning, and a practice that students from all backgrounds should have access and exposure to.

Middle-class families routinely ensure that their children have exposure to internships, camps, traveling, learning new skills, and deeper learning, all of which prepare them to make more informed choices about their likes and dislikes. Those expansive experiences can help all young people, as can familiarity with work, to understand and feel the positive connections to contributing to something larger than oneself. The data about teens and work are not on our side. As a recent Brooking Institution report discusses, "The teens with the highest employment rates come from families earning $120,000 or more, and the rates are lowest among teens with family incomes below $40,000, the young people most in need of earning power."[11]

What if we changed the call from "college for all" to "success and dignity for all, with the promise of earning a living wage" or, more succinctly, "college and/or career for all"?

BOSTON ARTS ACADEMY AND CAREER EDUCATION

When I became the founding headmaster of BAA, we focused on our college-acceptance rates. Six college presidents of local arts colleges had written the original "charter" for the school with the intention of bringing urban students from Boston to matriculate and obtain degrees from their institutions. These presidents, and other community members, had fought for over two decades to start an arts high school in the face of intense opposition. In the wake of court-ordered desegregation in Boston, many believed that an arts education was incompatible with college readiness and that a school that had auditions for admissions would create more segregation in an already troubled school system. We were determined to prove the skeptics wrong. Through a carefully developed recruitment system, BAA is one of the most racially and economically diverse schools in Boston.

As determined as we were for BAA to be a college preparatory arts high school, we also wanted to explore career and technical training for our students. So many arts-related fields are highly technical, such as lighting, sound, and even costume design. In fact, the very first grant we were awarded was to start a technical theater program. We wanted to ensure that our graduates would know "all aspects of the industry" (to use the vocational term) and thus would be well-rounded and employable artists. Our theater students needed to know how to both design and build the sets, for example, as well as act in or direct a play. The same was true in visual arts: not only would students learn to draw and paint, but they would develop the career and technical skill known as visual communications, which would give them access to the burgeoning field of graphic design.[12]

We have felt strongly, since day one, that our students deserved both an academic education and career and technical preparation. Our intention, always, was to debunk the assumption that there is an "either-or" between technical education on the one hand and humanities/arts on the other. Some of our students gained greatly from our methods. If a student showed real interest in lighting or set design, those teachers would use their connections to find internships at local theaters after school or during the summers. However, students were not required, as part of their sequential coursework, to do an internship. My discussions with BAA alumni make me wonder how we should expand our thinking and educational programming to be more explicit about career preparation. One of those alumni was Jason. Along with Trey, Martin, Eric, and Gwen, who are introduced later in the chapter, Jason has helped me reexamine my own assumptions about college for all.

LESSONS FROM BAA ALUMNI

Jason would moonwalk down the halls even though it was no longer "in" for most teens. He was always a blur of color and movement, embodying flair wherever he went by either adapting current hip-hop fashion trends or generating a completely new look others would eventually embrace. He'd combine bold plaids and stripes, sometimes even incorporating polka-dot socks into the mix, color coordinating with the newest sneakers on the market. Style and fashion meant everything to him.

I always looked forward to seeing Jason since I didn't know what era he'd be wearing or representing. One day, for instance, he came in with a big boom box like Radio Raheem, the character in Spike Lee's 1989 movie, *Do the Right Thing*. He was a visual arts major as committed to his sketchbook as he was to the recording studio. He laid down beats at the same time as he videotaped his best friends break-dancing. He dreamed of chronicling the life of his neighborhood through color, movement, and sound. Every month brought a different idea of a video he was going to make. And, if he wasn't going to be famous as a video artist, then he might have to become the leader of the next musical fad.

One of his best friends was Oscar. Where Jason was flashy and stylish with his dress, Oscar used his talents on his own head, cutting and shaving various emblems and messages into each new haircut. He had a successful side business with his peers from school and the neighborhood. One of their dreams was that Oscar would own his own barbershop, and Jason would make videotapes of kids getting signature haircuts. Oscar would cut the hair, Jason would shoot, edit, and score each video with an original soundtrack to advertise their unique business, as well as provide the parents with a fun documentary. Jason blended art and entrepreneurship in true hip-hop fashion. With plans after high school that involved making hit tunes and raps as well as videos, Jason didn't want college getting in the way of his creative endeavors.

"You all made college applications part of graduation," he said. "We had to apply. And we had to have plans. I guess I really felt that what I wanted to do didn't count." Jason was right. Our mantra was college for all or at least a clear career plan, in the military, a jobs program, or placement in a professional company. We pressured Jason not to just drift off to make videos at his neighborhood art center, make music at a local recording studio, or go into business with Oscar. We didn't disparage any of those professions; we just felt that our students needed a college degree to ensure future success and earnings.

By late spring, no matter how many times Jason's advisor sat with him to complete applications, he had still missed all the deadlines for colleges. "I wanted to go to Cooper Union or California Art Institute. I knew my portfolio was good. We had a portfolio class and everything, but by the time I looked into it all, I knew I'd never get a scholarship. And I couldn't figure out how I'd get there anyway. Everything seemed too far away and too hard." He agreed to visit a local community college.

After the visit, he got excited about all the video course offerings and the opportunity to transfer credits to the Massachusetts College of Art and Design, where he could major in video production and could cross register at Berklee College of Music and take sound engineering courses—and at the cost of a state college. It seemed like a good plan to him. But then some major changes shook his foundation. Just before graduation, his father left the house and his mother lost her job and decided she needed to move back down South to live with her mother. Jason opted for staying with his friend Oscar; he already had a job after school and helped pay for food and some rent. Even though he managed to graduate from high school and still had a plan to go on to community college, Jason felt pretty unsettled.

"My life kinda fell apart—really more like imploded. Even though Oscar's mom was cool with me staying there, I knew they had a lot going on in that house too. Oscar's mom was really disappointed that he wasn't going to college. And his plans to be a barber had kinda fallen through. I don't think either of us felt good about anything. But you know you don't talk much about that kind of thing. So, I did what I thought would be best—go to community college."

I saw Jason the first day of the semester when I happened to attend a meeting on his community college campus. He was still bursting with color and eye-catching chains and necklaces. But the community college environment wasn't like an arts high school. Classes were big and formal and based on lectures and textbooks. Jason felt out of place in what, to him, seemed like a big factory of people just trying to pass one class in order to get to the next. He didn't connect with anyone and felt that the classes were only repeating what he'd learned in high school. Jason didn't last the semester. He went back to working at the community arts center where he'd first gotten excited about video production. "I figured I might as well do what I was good at and not waste my time."

Jason has been working for over two years. When we talked recently, I asked him whether he wished he'd stayed in community college. "I couldn't have stayed there. It was just not what I wanted then. I needed to work, to really grow up and figure out my road and what I wanted to do. I'm earning okay here. I have an apartment with a roommate. I can pay my way. And I'm doing what I love. And I'm teaching kids like me. I realized that was what I was made to do."

I wanted to know about college. Was that in the future? "Well, I hope it is," he said. "But I have to want it. I have to be ready to receive it and be willing to work for that degree. I know you guys believed that pushing us all to go to college was the right thing to do. But I think for kids like me . . . Well, we have to figure it out on our own."

Jason acknowledged that he was a bit of a rebel in high school and more interested in hip-hop culture than anything else. "I wanted to make money in the hip-hop world. I wanted to make videos, create fashion, do graffiti. And I rapped and I was good at laying those sounds down. I wanted to tell the stories of my neighborhood and kids like me. College didn't seem the way to get there, but I didn't feel I could really say that and be heard. Everyone was applying. So finally that's what I did. But my heart wasn't in it."

I wondered how we could have better supported Jason as a senior. "I guess, not making me feel so pressured that college was the only way. I think it would help to meet people who had worked for a bunch of years and then went to college or who went to training programs instead of college. I'm thinking now about learning about electronics and stuff. I want to be able to fix things. I've always been good at that. But I didn't know anything about how you find those kind of programs. Since I've been working here, I've learned a lot more about that."

Jason's experience at BAA echoes quite a number of graduates. Trey, another BAA alumnus, says, "I went to college for a year because I really thought I had to. But I hated it. It was a waste of my time and money. I wish I had known more about careers while in high school. I wish I had been able to intern at a theater or something." Trey is now in Los Angeles acting professionally and seemingly on the verge of making a career of it. He's done television shows, films, and commercials. All of BAA lights up when he gets cast in another pilot! "I loved BAA. It will always be the best community and the best family of artists I could ever ask for, but I think two things would have helped: a class on the practicalities of the art world and more working artists as teachers. I just didn't know or believe that acting was a real career—and one I could get good at." Trey acknowledges that acting is incredibly hard work with an excruciatingly demanding schedule. But he also is happy to be doing what he loves. "I've got a working-life that I want, and that makes all the difference. College just isn't for everyone."

Will, another alumnus, tells me, "I'm thirty now, and I found college totally boring. I wanted to major in visual arts, but the content of the courses was what we had already studied in high school. I wanted to get out and work. Now I'm working for a car service company and I'm already making in the low sixties with good benefits, and I've had lots of promotions. Who knows where I'll go from here? But it took me a long time to stop feeling guilty for leaving college. At BAA, college was the only choice unless you were a professional dancer, and there weren't too many of us who were doing that." Will may have chosen the path best for him, and he may be the exception to the rule about future earnings and a college degree. Nevertheless, would he be promoted faster and would he have more opportunities with a degree?

Gwen, unlike some other alums I spoke to, found her college program to be very engaging and relevant to her field of choice, building on the technical skills she had acquired in high school. She was a theater major who became immersed in the world of lighting design. Her design teacher helped her secure summer internships doing installations for a variety of corporations as well as in local theaters. She struggled academically because she was an English Language learner with a dyslexia diagnosis. For a long time, she thought that she would work right after high school. After all, she had good technical skills and lots of experience (although not a vocational certificate). Gwen applied to only one college, a conservatory. She knew she could never afford it without a full scholarship, and she knew how competitive the spots were. She had decided that she would go to college only if tuition was paid for. But if not, she felt she had other options. Luckily for Gwen, she was given a full scholarship. "This is like being at work," she described her first year at college. "You are part of an ensemble with shows and deadlines just like in high school, but much more intense. And I get to do a lot of technical theater and in wonderful spaces with tons of equipment. It's like a four-year apprenticeship. I don't know if I'll be a professional actor or designer when I get through. But I will be something. And it all started with the kinds of practical experiences I got at BAA."

HOW WE COULD HAVE HELPED

Gwen's journey is what I had hoped for Jason and many others: that college would provide four years of extensive and immersive experiences that would prepare them for the world of work—and with a degree. As I reflect on the stories of my graduates I am struck by the binary choices they experience: college or work. Given that nearly a third of students won't go to college, should their only other choice be a low-paid job? What could high schools do to better support alternate pathways to a rewarding and dignified life? After hearing from my alums, I discussed this with my colleagues and we considered other possibilities.

What about a fifth year in high school with a full-time internship that would provide more opportunities for students to grow before committing to college? The aim would be for students to finish their high school requirements, but not graduate until they finished a supervised internship. Students would still apply to (and hopefully be accepted to) a college of their choice. They would receive financial aid and could apply for scholarships, but they would defer for a year in order to learn more about the world of work and hone their own passions. Of course this wouldn't make sense for everyone—especially those who apply and get into some of the more elite institutions with help from organizations like Posse. However, for other students, who are just going through the motions of applying for college, this extra year with additional support from a high school community that has deeply invested in them could add another year of maturity and help make college less of a maze. Students could even wait a year to apply to college.

The downside to this idea is that Massachusetts (like most other states) measures high schools' success by their four-year graduation rate. To fit within that mold, we might consider a complete revamping of the curriculum so that the final year of high school could include a full-time internship and dual enrollment in college courses. Still, so many of our students, who entered high school academically under-prepared, need those four years of intensive instruction, so this seems less feasible. Another idea proposed required summer coursework for everyone (BAA now has a summer reading program for rising tenth and eleventh graders). We discussed a more comprehensive orientation and skills program for rising ninth graders, but staffing and costs are always a concern. If college remains the goal for all of our students then we must create different pathways for achieving that. We will need the state to be flexible about its requirements, and the ways it labels and measures success, in order for schools to meet the needs of their diverse students.

Schools need opportunities and incentives to introduce more comprehensive pathways to connect and combine the world of work with academics. Evaluating schools through the one-dimensional lens of state test scores has greatly limited creative ways of engaging students, leaving no room in the curriculum for comprehensive career exploration. Schools are either vocational or comprehensive high schools. Students are clamoring for more variation in their high school education and vocational schools; at least in Massachusetts, many more students apply than can currently be accommodated.[13] The solution would be more integration of career and academic education. Some states, like New Hampshire, have introduced extended-learning opportunities, or ELOs, as a way of giving students opportunities to seek independent learning and more vocational or career experiences. Students can propose to a counselor or coordinator the idea of an internship in an area of interest, such as working for the Division of Fisheries and Wildlife, or the police department, but the process is totally student-driven and the requirements for connection back to the classroom are not systematic. This is, however, a step in the right direction. An advantage of this approach is that, if done well, vocational and academic education can support one another rather than being seen as a dual-tiered system. Many of these ideas about extending classroom experiences and connecting work experiences with schools have their roots in a movement that took shape in the mid-1980s.

SCHOOL-TO-WORK OR SCHOOL-TO-CAREER

Across the country, a new model called "school to work" was becoming widely known in the mid-1980s. Boston Public Schools, along with other districts, had experimented with schools where students studied in academic classes until midday and then went to work. To avoid confusion with vocational programs, school-to-work quickly became known as school-to-career. School-to-career programming demonstrated a connection between work experiences and coursework, and by the mid-1980s, it had become a well-supported idea in education. Fenway High School, then called the Fenway Program, was an early adherent.

Fenway High School, which was originally a program of English High School, sat across the street from Boston Latin School, right in the middle of the famous Boston hospitals located along Longwood Avenue. Harvard Medical School students ate lunch in a cafeteria right next door, and Children's Hospital was across the street. Our students and the hospital employees walked the same streets to get to their respective morning "jobs," but their lives were often worlds apart. "School to work" sought to change this.

Much of the work we did at Fenway High School in the 1980s and 1990s involved developing school-to-career pathways for students. At first, we only had one partner, the John Hancock Insurance Company. The company had annually provided a "back to school" event for teachers, where we were invited to their famous top floor to marvel at the city below us and given delicious hors d'oeuvres. The business leaders were saying thank you to us for the hard work that lay ahead. For a couple of years, the company also sent tutors by the busload to our school. Given this prior relationship, and the rising tensions in the city related to the growth of gangs, drugs, and increasing poverty in many neighborhoods, the mayor was asking businesses to do more for young people in the form of job training. The company agreed to begin an aggressive jobs program with us and offer entry-level jobs and internships to our students. The number of John Hancock department heads who wanted to be involved in helping to train our students was remarkable since this certainly took time away from their own work. Yet, these department heads believed that bringing in city kids to learn from and work with them would not only benefit the bottom line but would also be the right thing to do for the culture of the entire company.

Students needed a minimum B- average to be considered for after-school and summer employment. They had to write an application, get a recommendation from a teacher, and be interviewed by a Hancock employee. For the twenty-five slots, at least double that number of qualified students applied. An added feature of the program was a class that all student employees took. Cindy, who worked in human resources and had at one time harbored a desire to be a teacher, taught the class with me. Some weeks the class was at the high school and some weeks at the job site.

We read various cases and books about work (such as Studs Terkel's classic 1974 text *Working*) and reflected in writing about the work experiences described. We discussed similarities and differences of those experiences with the students. We also discussed race and class, never wanting to ignore the fact that most John Hancock employees were white and from more middle-class backgrounds than our students. However, we knew that our students could find ways to feel comfortable at the company and pave the way for a more diverse work force. The goal of the class was to help students discern their own strengths and challenges, as well as to increase reading, writing, and speaking skills.

Cindy couldn't have been more different from our students. She lived in the suburbs and rarely interacted with others from a different racial or socio-economic background, but she brought an energy and commitment to the partnership that I marveled at. She suggested readings and assignments and even wanted to correct student papers. She would encourage students to come see her for special office hours so she could help improve their writing skills. In the class, students had an opportunity to discuss job situations that were confusing or for which they felt unprepared. Cindy helped create an atmosphere where students spoke candidly about their frustrations. Many of their previous jobs had been either working at fast food restaurants or bagging groceries where, if there were disagreements, the students just quit, rather than working through it with a supervisor or learning to take criticism. Much of our curriculum involved understanding how to "hear" another's point of view and not just react. Being courteous, pleasant, and on time were all part of the job training. We also had to talk about the dress code, and Cindy was masterful at that. One day she came in with big earrings like many of our students wore, and they looked at her with amazement. What was she doing dressed like that? She grinned and said, "I was going to ask you all the same thing!" She had made her point.

Students were placed into various departments in the company, such as accounts, payroll, and human resources, and even as assistants to higher level staff. In addition to working with our students, John Hancock employees continued to regularly come to the school to serve as tutors and volunteers in other capacities. For our students, the benefits of this partnership were numerous. Not only were they working and earning money, which was much needed in their families, but their job experiences gave them opportunities to develop interpersonal skills as well as problem-solving skills. Talking about problem solving in math or science is one thing; having the pressure of a job in which solving a problem accurately or quickly might make a huge difference is quite another. Students felt valued for their expertise and insights. They knew that when they did a good job, they made the work easier for their supervisors. The relationship that students developed with their John Hancock mentor or boss often was sustained long after the internship ended. Numerous individuals, like Cindy, insisted that students work on their college applications at the Hancock offices, and many wrote letters of recommendation for them.

Sonya, one of our students who started off in payroll, worked at the company part-time all the way through college. I saw her recently at Boston City Hall where she has worked ever since college. "Yeah, I started running things in high school when I worked my way up at John Hancock, remember?" Sonya jogged my memory. She had started filing papers, then secured an internship with the head of the department and eventually was offered a full-time job. She went to college part-time for years and then became a city employee with excellent benefits and even more responsibility running a high-level office.

Based on the success of this work, Fenway expanded its program to partner with Children's Hospital. Now, instead of twenty-five students in off-site work experiences, we had nearly double. A hospital is quite different from an insurance company, and we wanted our students to have exposure in as many different areas as possible. We developed rotations in nutrition, human resources, IT, and phlebotomy, and even had students working in the design and architectural department as well as the president's office at the hospital's not-for-profit foundation. The funding came both from the hospital and from a citywide entitlement program where tax-exempt institutions, in lieu of taxes, sponsored community-based initiatives. The hospital's commitment to the growth and development of our students was remarkable. They were our physical neighbors and recognized that many of their patients lived in the very same communities as our students, which brought mutual benefit because Children's had few employees from these neighborhoods. The hospital needed culturally competent employees and recognized that an early investment in teenagers could pay off later. Our young students needed jobs and experiences that would help them positively access adult role models and mentors. Many of those students today are leading successful middle-class lives working as phlebotomists in hospitals, computer technicians, pharmacists, or police officers. Others have gone on to college.[14]

I recently received an e-mail from Jaclyn, who reminisced about her years both in high school and beyond as a phlebotomist. She remembered the initial suspicion that the department head felt over hiring a high school senior. "But I was always on time, always willing to learn and do extra things, and pretty soon she forgot that I was in high school. I am very grateful for those experiences. I'm now working as a hospital administrator in Florida."

One of the ways we deepened our understanding of the possibilities of school-to-career programming came from a trip to Denmark. Jobs for the Future is a national not-for-profit organization that specializes in providing strategic assistance and research to schools and districts involved in school and work partnerships. It sponsored a trip to Denmark for over a dozen American educators from across the country whose schools were experimenting with school-to-career programs. We had the chance to meet with young people and employers, to understand their long-standing and deep commitment to vocational education and apprenticeship learning.

We visited general education high schools, vocational high schools, and the famed Lego factory, which sponsored some of the most sophisticated and competitive apprenticeships for youth. From our conversations we learned that the vocational schools were not seen as "less than" the general education schools. In fact, for many young people, getting into a vocational school meant that you were almost guaranteed a good job. It also did *not* mean you couldn't attend university. As one young person said to us, "At this [vocational] school, the teachers understand that we learn best by doing and making things." The visit strengthened my understanding of the importance of adolescents experiencing a working-life along with more traditional academic courses. After this trip, Fenway began developing its "house" system in which all students would experience some connection to work, as well as a six-week full-time senior internship.

Fenway evolved and embraced new career pathways and partnerships. In the 1990s, the school was divided into three distinct "houses," each with an employer partner: Children's Hospital, CVS Pharmacies, and the Museum of Science. Each partner provided jobs, mentoring, and a commitment to our school. At least one senior member of each outside institution joined our school-site-council or board and helped the school hone its strategic directions and mission. As part of our collaborative work, the school evolved from offering a weekly work-readiness class to creating a fully developed internship program for seniors. Seniors spent six weeks full time at a job site and completed a comprehensive research paper about the company or organization along with reflections about their own personal growth and development. In addition, most students also took an entrepreneurship class so that they could begin to understand how businesses operated. As a concluding celebratory and introspective activity at the end of the Senior Internship, mentors would join students at a breakfast hosted by the school. This provided the opportunity for students to speak about their experiences as well as to thank their mentors, who could choose to talk about their student employee.

I will never forget listening to Teresa, an employer, speak about her mentee. What was most remarkable is that Teresa was a Fenway graduate and in the first class of our internship program. "When I was at Fenway, I didn't know what I wanted to do. There were gangs and drugs all around me and my neighborhood. Just getting to school was an accomplishment. But I was given the chance to intern at a legal firm, and it changed my world. I wanted to go to college. I wanted to be in the legal profession. In large part that was due to my supervisor, who I am still in touch with."

Fenway figured out how to be both a rigorous academic institution and one that provided serious opportunities for students to apprentice in a job site and build lasting adult relationships. Fenway is often credited as piloting some of the earliest career and technical education programs without having the official federal "vocational education" designation. I mention this because vocational programs are budgeted at a much higher per pupil amount. Vocational programs also include sequential coursework in a specific pathway such as allied health or graphic design that helps students understand "all aspects of the industry." As importantly, vocational classes are taught by a certified vocational teacher who has had work experience in his or her field. Even without that assistance, Fenway provided excellent work experiences with opportunities for support and reflection along with a four-year college preparatory curriculum. Fenway intended to better prepare students for entering college by giving them experiences in the real world. These work experiences had the added advantage of sometimes creating a career pathway for a student.

We certainly want more students to interact with possible careers while in high school. If these work experiences can also connect to high-quality coursework, whether offered at the high school level or a neighboring community college, or even online, students will have more opportunities to become immersed and knowledgeable in a field. This doesn't pigeonhole a student into a career, but gives students more opportunities to explore (and discard) possible interests while gaining valuable work-place skills.

The balance of career and technical education with academic education ought to be the goal of many more schools today. Shawsheen Vocational Regional Technical High School is another success with many ways to lead us forward.

GETTING IT RIGHT: SHAWSHEEN

Charles Lyons, former superintendent of Shawsheen Vocational Regional Technical High School in Billerica, Massachusetts, insists that vocational, or career and technical education serves an important need in American education and society. He feels strongly that our national priorities have gone awry. "When you hear 'college for all,' I think that's a bunch of crap. There is little correlation between a college degree and career success. I took a look at UMass–Amherst graduates a few years ago, and out of a graduating class of approximately 5,000, 1,500 students received degrees in the social sciences with majors such as sociology, anthropology, and women's studies; 150 received engineering degrees. Those social scientists will make great waiters, waitresses, and conversationalists, but they aren't prepared for jobs."

Lyons may be being sarcastic, but I understand his point of view as someone who has fought for decades to get vocational education to be seen as on par with general education and not a "less-than" track. For Lyons, career exploration is worthwhile, but does not go far enough. The cornerstone of effective career and technical programs is a cooperative (co-op) experience for juniors and seniors to ensure that the students are actually working while they are in high school. As he said to me, "We graduate twenty-six electricians a year. They receive over 1,500 hours of work in their junior year. This means that a master electrician can employ them in their senior year. They can have 2,400 hours when they walk out this door. They know they need 8,000 [hours]. They *know* whether they want to go right to work and continue working for a master electrician or go to UMass–Lowell and pursue an electrical engineering degree."

For Lyons, the role of high schools is to help students make an informed decision about work and college. He doesn't want vocational schools to create caste systems in education, yet he feels that high schools have an obligation to open up the world of work. Lyons is incensed by the "college for all" mantra. He argues that it's elitist and constantly promoted by everyone who already went to college. "What about people who want to work with their hands? What about people who want to contribute to a local economy? You still need plumbers, electricians, mail carriers, and car mechanics." Many of those jobs require considerable competence because the technology is so advanced. And many of those jobs require coursework and some college after high school, but not a four-year degree.

Paul Harrington, a researcher from the Center for Labor Studies at Drexel University, believes that career and technical education is key to success in high school and beyond. When high school is a combination of student exploration with varied experiences and teacher or peer instruction, young people will engage more deeply. Like many of today's well-known cognitive psychologists and learning scientists, Harrington argues that young people need to ask and answer, "What do I like to do? What am I good at?" Harrington believes that high school ought to be a place where those questions and answers can be tested against the labor market. Work experience, he argues, is where the most important things in the job market—social skills such as the ability to persuade, interact, negotiate—are key indicators of how one will survive and thrive. For many young people, work experience is the first time they have an adult relationship outside of the family or school, and they feel responsible about their contributions to a company or a job. In fact, work experience is an essential aspect of the transition into adulthood. Economic self-sufficiency and an understanding of one's possible contributions to the larger society are critical components of positive self-development. We knew that in the early 1980s at Fenway High School when we developed programs with John Hancock. And we saw the positive effects on our students. I saw much of the same when I visited Shawsheen.

Shawsheen serves many middle- and working-class communities just outside the city of Boston. Approximately 92 percent of Shawsheen's students are white; 4 percent are Hispanic; less than 2 percent are African American; and 2 percent are not categorized.[15] About 25 percent are classified as special needs; approximately 13 percent are economically disadvantaged, which is the federal term used to describe students who are eligible for free and reduced lunch. About 32 percent of the students are described as high needs. In the new reauthorization of the Elementary and Secondary Education Act of 2016, high needs include all students who are English language learners, require special education, or are economically disadvantaged. (In most urban districts, the percentage of high-needs students can be well over 80 percent, with some reaching 100 percent.)

When I arrived at Shawsheen, I immediately noted the somewhat lackluster facility. The low-slung building boasted a sign that looked as if it hadn't been refurbished for some years. The lobby, although lined with glass cases filled with a number of trophies and awards, wasn't particularly impressive. However, as I visited shops and classes, and talked with students and teachers, I was struck by the maturity and excitement of the students and the depth of their experiences in applied learning. Shops and studios were all well-lit and well furnished, demonstrating the school's priorities.

One freshman, after rotating through many shop experiences during the first nine months of school, reflected realistically, "Using college as a place to grow up is very expensive. I'm glad that I have gotten exposed to lots of different areas I might want to specialize in since school started. I thought I wanted to be a nurse. But I really like art. I like making stuff. So I've chosen graphic design as my pathway. I'll be studying here for the next three years." When I asked if she thought she'd go to college, she didn't miss a beat, saying, "I hope so. But I'll be able to work while I'm in college. I see what the juniors and seniors are doing when they go out to their job placements as part of their co-ops. They get paid well in great companies." This young woman would be certified in commercial art and graphic design. She would also know how to use many different design programs, such as Adobe Illustrator, and she would have experience developing materials for companies and clients. If she were selected for a co-op in her junior year, she would spend one full week every other week out on a job. She certainly did not view her vocational education as "less than" what her peers received in "regular" high school. In fact, she was proud to have had to interview with a guidance counselor as part of her entrance into the school. "You have to want to be here otherwise it doesn't make sense."

Teachers concurred with this sentiment and talked about how what they teach not only prepares students to succeed in a particular field, but also reinforces academic concepts. For example, in carpentry the light bulb often went off for students when introduced to the Pythagorean theorem. Suddenly, students realized that what they were learning in math class was critical for building a house correctly. The shop teacher related a recent interaction with a student who proclaimed, "I like this math and the way we do it here." As the teacher explained, this was a student who learned through doing and not just problem sets.

I wondered about the level or intensity of collaborative work between shop and academic teachers. Each employs a distinct approach to teaching concepts, but both would benefit from more sharing of pedagogy. This had been one of the great hopes of the school-to-career movement—the idea that experiential learning could become mainstream. Sadly, when high-stakes testing became the norm, experiential learning took a back seat.

Mickey was graduating from allied health as a certified nursing assistant. He was proud of his accomplishments but knew from his exposure to the field that he wasn't interested in patient care. "I'm glad I was able to learn while in high school what I like and what I don't like," he said. "A teacher said in my freshman year, 'If you love what you do, you'll never work a day in your life.'" Mickey explained that he didn't love patients and yet that's the work of nurses. "I found out that I loved the science of the field—doing the analysis of the blood or the urine, but not the 'hands-on' part with people." Mickey had been accepted to a local university and was planning on majoring in clinical lab science. "I want to know what causes diseases and work in labs. That's much more interesting to me than people." He grinned at his teacher as he spoke. "Yes, I know. I like order and processes. Humans aren't predictable and that's scary for me."

I had a hard time believing I was talking to a seventeen-year-old who had such clarity about his passions and future plans. This ability to reflect was repeated as I talked to students about their experiences, whether in electrical, plumbing, cosmetology, culinary, dental, or design shops. The opportunities to learn "applied theory," related to their vocational studies, coupled with paid work experiences, had given these young people confidence to enter an uncertain world. One student, aptly nicknamed Chance, said, "I probably won't be a plumber in the future, but I know I'll always be able to fix things in my house and I'm proud of that." Chance was leaving the next day for his co-op work experience. "I'm excited and also nervous. It's my first time getting paid to work and I know how important it is that I do well. How I perform will reflect on my classmates who are coming behind me."

Students at Shawsheen are grateful for their academic, vocational, and career preparation. Their teachers, no matter what disciplines they teach, also are excited, much like those at BAA, to have students who elected to be at the school. The vocational teachers, in particular, are proud of their students' potential. The instructors understand that, while not all students will pursue a field in their designated pathway, learning skills and knowledge in fields like plumbing, dentistry, or graphic design will have positive repercussions for life choices later on. Students gain confidence as they become experts in one area, and that confidence is transferable to learning another skill or to making the decision to pursue college.

LEARNING FROM INTERNATIONAL EXAMPLES

Nancy Hoffman, author and researcher with Jobs for the Future, suggests the United States borrow from some of the successes of the Nordic countries and other postindustrial nations such as Singapore, Germany, and Switzerland.[16] In Switzerland, for example, students experience a more cohesive approach to education and work. It's not, "First get your education and then go to work." At least two-thirds of sixteen- to nineteen-year-olds are involved in vocational education. One of the hallmarks of the Swiss system is its permeability. Students can choose either a practical or theoretical apprenticeship, but they are not locked out of a future academic education if they choose a practical one. "About 40 percent of 15-year-olds who score a 4 or 5 on PISA (i.e., the top end of the range on this international test) choose vocational education, signaling that apprenticeship is a high status way to learn," writes Hoffman.[17] The Swiss Vocational Education and Training (VET) system competes with university training. Young people choose between two equally well-funded and well-respected pathways. Vocational education is seen as the best way to enter careers in IT, finance, banking, and child care. The Swiss education system continues to modernize and add fields that can be studied through VET as opposed to attending university. Dance, music, elder care, and engineering were recently added to the more traditional trades and fields such as advanced manufacturing, which have always been VET concentrations. One of the hallmarks of the VET system is its commitment to the "teaching of metacognition, providing students with regular opportunities to discuss what they are learning and why they are learning it."[18] Students are able to describe the three pillars of vocational education: know, know how to, and apply. Furthermore, as Hoffman notes, the school, the training company, and the workplace all work collaboratively to ensure future success for students. "The Swiss curriculum documents are laid out with very clear goals, outcomes and activities for each of the VET settings."[19]

When I visited a vocational school in Iceland, I was first struck by the high quality of the shops and equipment. Students, as Hoffman described in her research, were very clear about why they had chosen this school as opposed to a more standard baccalaureate secondary education. As one student in a machine shop class said, "I like reading manuals, probably more than I like reading novels. And I want to fix things. I've always liked school, but the chance to do school and work is a perfect combination for me." The student was learning to repair tractors and other large machines and would graduate with the ability to go right to work.

The teachers worked on the shop floor with students preparing them for the next semester when they would apprentice for the tractor company. One teacher commented, "Our students here may go on to a polytechnic or even a university, and we give them a chance to think about which is the best path for them. Right now they need to connect work experiences to what I'm teaching. You can't just repair an engine, let's say, without seeing why it's critical to do a perfect job." Students understood that if they made even a small error it would cost somebody else time and money.

I also visited the recording and design studios where students were either prepping for an upcoming radio broadcast or finishing a design presentation for a local firm. One young man planned to major in broadcast journalism in the future and he knew his show would be part of his portfolio for admission. His classmate, a smartly dressed young woman, was preparing for her industry presentation. The teacher explained to me that a variety of design firms would come to the school to critique student work and then make decisions about offering jobs or unpaid internships. Part of the curriculum involved reading short stories and novels and then creating a visual storyboard. "We want our designers to be well-read and have many ideas to draw from," the teacher said. "This is not just a technical field but a creative one." Students in both the broadcast and design tracks could enroll in a large selection of academic classes since their school shared a campus with a more traditional high school. Students were given a great deal of flexibility in putting together a program of study that balanced academic high school requirements and vocational ones and didn't track them into "just being in design."

The Swiss system bears out much of what we tried to implement over twenty years ago at Fenway, but we lacked school district and national policy support. The Swiss seem to emulate "deeper learning," the current term du jour to describe what schools should be doing to connect in-school and out-of-school experiences. The fact that the two systems are seen as equally competitive and rigorous completely changes expectations at the secondary-school level. Imagine if American high school students knew that they could study careers in music or finance in a vocational school as either an alternative or precursor to college. Imagine if our community colleges could truly reinvent themselves and be places where students enter the allied health professions or even design professions.

Even though Germany's system is much more tracked than in Switzerland, and they do a poor job with immigrant and poor students, we can still learn from its emphasis on career and technical education. They have an impressive history of employers developing competitive apprentice programs that allow many young people to enter the middle class without a college degree. For example, the Bayer company runs an apprenticeship program where students get onsite training combined with studies at a technical college.[20] There is no stigma associated with these kinds of programs, since they so clearly support entry into the middle class.

Although the US educational system fundamentally differs from other countries', we need to note successes in other parts of the world and begin to borrow some ideas and strategies to improve our own outcomes.

RACE AND CAREER AND TECHNICAL EDUCATION

We should continue our vigilance about tracking and CTE education. And, we must pay attention to how lack of funding and attention to quality staffing can harm our young people. When Madison Park Career and Technical High School was founded in 1980 as the Hubert Humphrey Occupational Resource Center, the facility held such promise for both young people and adults in Boston. Its location, in the heart of the black community, was heralded as an opportunity for many new jobs that would come to Boston's Roxbury neighborhood. Unfortunately, enrollment and budget troubles plagued the school from the start. As we've explored in the examples of Shawsheen and other successful programs, certain elements are necessary for success: well-equipped, up-to-date facilities; qualified and vocationally certified teachers who know the industry well and can form lasting relationships with employers and unions; and students who have chosen to be there. When I studied Madison Park as part of an evaluation team in 2014, little of that was in place.

In the hotel and tourism classes, students worked on assignments downloaded from some Internet site. When, during a visit, I asked students if they hoped to go into this industry, they looked at me blankly. "This is just a class we have to pass. We don't really want to be here," one boy told me. He was doing a cost-benefit analysis of whether a hotel chain should expand. I thought, maybe, that would be a good thing to know if you were running a hotel. "How could I ever run a hotel?" the young student said to me. "I would need to learn so many things I'm not learning here. We never even get to work in one." The young man was trying to be polite. "Here in our 'lab' [he used air quotes], we learn to make beds and clean a fake hotel room. That's what my mother does for work every night."

Successful vocational programs are evaluated on the number of students who successfully enter and complete co-op. (Of course this depends on the faculty's ability to create and sustain co-op programs.) Without this experience, students could not actually earn a vocational certificate. The fact that so few students actually did work outside of the school should have sounded alarm bells early on.

The marked difference between Shawsheen's and Madison Park's facilities and co-ops mirror a marked difference in their geography and demographics. Shawsheen is suburban and predominately white, while Madison is urban with 92 percent students of color. Eighty-five percent of the student population is considered high need, compared with 72 percent in the school district. Over 37 percent are identified as special needs, and the district average is about 20 percent.[21] It is clear that the students in Roxbury were being severely underserved relative to their district peers. Persistent systematic inequality has plagued Madison Park almost since its inception.

However, another urban school offers a welcome counterpoint. More diverse than either of the previous examples, Worcester Technical High School (where 37 percent of students are white, 57 percent are high needs, and 12 percent receive special education services) is successful enough to have captured the attention of President Obama, who gave the 2014 commencement address there. He came to praise this school—its leadership and students—for truly creating a model of American competitiveness in the global economy. Vocational-technical high schools like Worcester's boast much lower dropout rates than traditional high schools across the state. For the 2013–14 academic year, the dropout rate at regional vo-techs was just 0.7 percent, nearly one-third of the rate at traditional public high schools in Massachusetts.[22] And the data for graduation rates for students with special needs from vocational-technical schools is also twenty-four points higher than at regular schools.

Worcester was not always a success story. In 2006, the school was the city's lowest-performing high school, but by 2014, 82 percent of graduates planned to enter two- or four-year colleges.[23] One of the most powerful ingredients for student success was the school's commitment to a curriculum that alternated between traditional academics and hands-on work in their trades. In addition, the school made a concerted effort to ensure the co-op experience, so foundational in career and technical schools. On the school's website, the third bullet is "education for equity in both the classroom and the work place."[24] Worcester lives this ethos through its curriculum and student experiences.

When I visited the school, I couldn't get over the gleaming modern facility and the sense of purpose shown by the students and faculty. I caught up with a few students who were walking back up the hill from their co-op in the local health clinic and asked if they planned to enter the health-care field. One girl nodded emphatically. "I'm so glad I've found what I love to do as a junior in high school. I'm going into nursing for sure." Another shook her head negatively. "I'm glad I've had this experience. I won't waste my time in college studying something I ultimately won't want. I'm going to intern this summer in the hospital's IT and development departments and see if that's what I like." I was curious if that was part of her CTE program. "No," she told me, "but my teacher wants to be sure I get some experiences before my senior year, so she helped me figure out who to talk to." This interchange stood in sharp contrast to conversations and observations at Madison. I am sure there are students at Madison for whom the education has been valuable, but as a rule, the city and the school department have not invested in that school to ensure its success.

IDEAS FOR THE FUTURE

Jason's story represents many BAA graduates who feel the intense pressure to go to college, while not convinced that path is right for them. We have not, as a nation, committed to the career part in the mantra "college and career for all." But we must. A continued redesign and reinvestment in the American high school must move us to a point where all students are afforded work and internship experiences. Our schools can be institutions where students can learn and practice democratic values, as well as places where they become better prepared to make life choices about future careers. We have seen how to bridge the purposes of school to include both the education for the common good and for career success. These need not be opposing forces. We just need the will to prioritize both.

Current federal policies and practices push us to organize our high schools and all of pre-K–12 education so that the largest numbers of young people will go to college. After hearing the stories of so many of my alumni, I've concluded that that laudable goal is no longer realistic or necessary. A student's future should not be reduced to the two alternatives of either a four-year degree or a service job. We know that at least a third of our nation's students will not get a four-year degree, so we owe them alternative pathways to a dignified life. For our students to become fully educated citizens, with a clear sense of how to access good jobs, we need a policy shift to *career* and college for all. This must be a sustainable policy transformation and not simply individual programs that rely on the good will of a particular director or favorable political winds. We need substantial investments and incentives to reintroduce career and technical education in middle and high school.

Here are some ideas that deserve further consideration.

1. *Deeper reinvestment in community colleges*

   Many community colleges pair with high school career pathways so that students earn both college credit and work experience. The work at Charlestown High School with Bunker Hill Community College is evidence of this. Students are now on an IT pathway where they take vocational classes together at the high school—in preparation for a work internship and college classes at the community college. This is a return to the "school-to-work" programs of the 1980s, but with a strong academic focus too. An added benefit is that these students travel as a cohort, get to know each other very well, and provide support to one another in their classes and internships. Springfield Technical Community College, another school that functions as a career training center, has been more successful with graduation rates. With community colleges as viable career starting places, more students would be better able to navigate life after high school.

2. *Focus on competency-based colleges*

   Competency-based college education may prove, over time, to be an important innovation for some students, and it has business support. Corporations that want their workers to advance in the industry with further education have partnered enthusiastically with College for America. But these programs should be clearly re-branded as "professional career and technical education" and not promise a college degree comparable to other four-year institutions.

3. *Acknowledge and incorporate success*
   - The Shawsheen and Worcester vocational technical schools are thriving in our state. Grow their models. Invest in career and technical education.
   - Linked Learning Alliance, the California-based initiative in which all students take both college-prep and career-prep classes, is working and has growth goals that are materializing.[25] Let's find ways to incorporate aspects of this model elsewhere in the country.
   - Lesson2Life pairs local businesses, service organizations, and chambers of commerce with classrooms and teachers so that teachers can voluntarily learn more about workplace skills and how to embed them in their curriculum. The teachers have access to personnel in a variety of industries, such as hospitality, the arts, nonprofits, large businesses, and startups.
   - Citizens Schools also pairs working professionals with middle schools to give students exposure to jobs and other career pathways they may not have ever considered.
   - Apprentice Learning, Inc., a local Boston nonprofit, works the opposite way. Instead of bringing employees into the school on a regular basis, this organization places eighth-grade students directly into internships, ensuring a "real world" learning experience in a variety of jobs and giving students an opportunity to practice workplace skills early in their lives and gain greater sense of future possibilities for themselves.

4. *Continue innovating*
   - Prepare all teachers, vocational and academic, to teach content in ways that fully engage students. Practice more hands-on project-based education.
   - Consider expanding extended-learning opportunities (ELOs), currently being piloted in the state of New Hampshire, in

which students gain academic credit for a variety of fieldwork. Ensure that this fieldwork connects clearly to reading, writing, and other academic skills.

5. *Teen jobs programs*
   Ensure that all eligible teens have summer jobs that help them realize pathways for a productive future. Ensure that there is no longer a racial and economic divide in who gets summer jobs.

6. *A new kind of Service Year for all Americans.*
   Instead of a Teach for America, I envision a kind of national Peace Corps that might be a massively scaled-up Lesson2Life, Citizen Schools, or Apprentice Learning. Working professionals, from actors to engineers, would be more deeply engaged in our schools and provide many opportunities for internships and mentoring. While in high school, young people choose to apprentice in a few different fields, such as child care and IT. Also, as with the John Hancock employees in the 1980s, businesses embrace their obligation to provide oversight and supervision to those young people. Furthermore, all young people, between high school and college, can be placed in a full-year paid internship to give them experience and exposure to circumstances and careers that would otherwise elude them.

The clarity and passion with which Mickey, at Shawsheen, spoke about his career choices were a product of his school's commitment to providing a structure where students can explore the world of work and answer those questions of "what am I good at, and what do I like to do?" As I've made the journey from Jason's story to Mickey's, I've come to believe we need a stronger commitment to CTE as a possible alternative to college. We need to reconsider what choice and passion might do for students, and we must structure high school experiences so that we can allow room for both. Then, and only then, can we imagine a world with schools that prepare our young people to be both college and career ready.

CHAPTER FIVE

"If You Believe, Your Dreams Will Come True"

All the assumptions I've discussed so far have some truth to them, which is why they came up in so many conversations with my alumni. But I now believe that the false promises embedded in these assumptions cause more harm than good for society. Throughout the previous chapters, I have suggested ways in which both high schools and colleges might ameliorate the obstacles to success encountered by many of our students.

The assumption I want to explore here is no less fraught with caveats, but in this case I want to focus on those students for whom the dream did in fact become reality: First, to celebrate their extraordinary achievements, while acknowledging the danger in holding up the exception as the rule. Second, and more importantly, to focus on what it means for students to "believe in their dreams" and how high schools can support all students in allowing this belief to flourish.

In interviews, my alumni recounted many powerful and ultimately positive experiences. As I listened to them, I was struck by how ardently they expressed some version of the idea that "if you just believe, your dreams will come true." They were not talking about belief in an abstract way; they were talking about belief in one's self—one's own agency and ability to succeed—even in the face of extraordinary obstacles. While chapter 3, "Just Work Harder," profiled alumni who faced many obstacles to success, in this chapter my intent is to explore the kind of education that might bolster this belief in one's own ability to succeed. One of the central questions for this chapter, then, is, What can schools do to empower students to believe in their own agency? I believe (as do many other educators) that schools can play a role in increasing students' determination, even though I do not believe in the pursuit of grit, in and of itself, as an educational panacea. Schools can create curricular conditions where young people practice and experience the deep work of long-term projects that require determination and also engage students in ongoing exploration. Imagine a curriculum that is structured in such a way as to strengthen students' sense of self and their sense of inclusion in a supportive community. This can help young people develop a positive sense of agency and belonging—both important conditions for beneficial personal and collective development.

This chapter follows some of BAA's most famous alumni, individuals who have "made it" in television and world-renowned dance companies, as well as other alumni who, although less well known, are enjoying impressive careers in the arts and other fields. They have proven that dreams *can* come true. All of these alumni have deeply believed in this maxim, and it has served them well. They are the poster children for achievement. They embody, in many respects, the tropes that feed the American dream for other young people and, really, for all of us.

The stories in this chapter are filled with optimism and hope. They are life-affirming stories that need to be told. The danger in focusing on such success stories, however, is that they reinforce the false impression, promulgated in the media, that given enough determination (or grit), every student, no matter how disadvantaged, can overcome large and oftentimes overwhelming obstacles. As with the other assumptions examined here, the few examples that validate this belief make it more likely we'll attribute failure to personal flaws or shortcomings or to the lack of sufficient grit, rather than pointing to the systemic inequities that can derail the dreams of even the most determined students.

In chapter 3, I focused on hard work and its limitations. But here I want to talk about what underlies individual perseverance. People will only work hard for goals they believe they can reach. They must believe in their abilities, their potential to improve those abilities, the worthiness of their goal, and the value of their contributions. As one BAA alumnus, Diego, an actor who later became a firefighter, commented on his life in the arts, "All of us had to believe we had something special to offer the world. Otherwise you couldn't do that hard work every day."

BAA has found some important ways to build into the school culture perseverance and the belief in oneself. This chapter will examine three of those strategies: (1) the integration of role models into many aspects of the school; (2) the creation of a strong, consistent community and culture; and finally (3) the capstone Senior Grant Project that gives students a structure whereby they can realize their own abilities to act and make change in their communities—however students define that. Although the way we implemented these strategies was specific to BAA and its arts focus, they can be applied to any school.

Through introducing students to successful "artists, scholars, and citizens" (BAA mission statement) who look like them and come from similar backgrounds, students see that their hard work can result in the career of their dreams. This is crucial to helping students own a narrative that is counter to the dominant one which says you can't be successful if you are poor, black or brown, or an immigrant or undocumented. Through both short- and long-term arts residencies, students regularly work with these role models. In academic classes as well, teachers strive to introduce their students to mathematicians, engineers, philosophers, and writers who share their struggles and successes. For example, Ty, from chapter 3, had met individuals from the National Society of Black Engineers while in his high school science class. Many schools have regular career days in which students are introduced to a host of jobs, industries, and people they may be unfamiliar with, and students are also encouraged to visit job sites and even arrange for internships. There are myriad nonprofit organizations that arrange for community or business people to come into schools for either a short-term visit or a longer residency. The point is this: young people need exposure and role models in order to help them imagine a different future.

Again and again the message at BAA is that we are not celebrating "exceptions." These individuals, both from the community and alumni, whose framed pictures adorn the walls of the BAA main office, are people just like our students. Much of BAA's curriculum now revolves around visiting artists so that students can see their own struggles to succeed reflected in professionals. In any given year, over twenty diverse artists work with students. Moreover, now that so many alumni are working in various industries, they continually return home to talk about their experiences. One such alumnus stands out.

Kirven Boyd began dancing with the Alvin Ailey Dance Company as soon as he graduated from high school. After eleven years as a principal dancer, Kirven stepped down at the age of thirty to begin his career as a teacher and choreographer. In his last year with Alvin Ailey, he returned to BAA to do a choreography residency. Students loved working with him; they acknowledged that he was strict and exacting, but also fun and funny. More than anything, they knew he was one of them. He is reflective about his experiences. "Kids, especially young dancers, appreciate being around people like me [and my husband] who grew up like them, who know what it's like to have to work hard for everything. And it's important that we are there for them. We are role models. How many black men are there that get where we have gotten? That's real. And it's important that young people know there is a way forward."

When I saw Kirven's dance performed by current BAA students, I knew he was right: he is a role model. As I took a picture of the dancers and Kirven after the performance, those young people knew that they had been touched by stardom, but I also knew that Kirven had given all of us an enormous gift: he had passed on his knowledge and his skills in a way that few of us would ever forget.

Not only alums but many other professionals share their time and stories with our students. Community members know that BAA students dream big, and at graduations and on various other occasions throughout the year, they come and validate those dreams. I recall Ron Crutcher, then president of Wheaton College in Norton, Massachusetts, who spoke at graduation. He told his story of the path that resulted in his position leading a small college that many of our graduates have aspired to attend. Then he sat down to perform for the students and family members in attendance. President Crutcher is a professional cellist. When he finished, the hall erupted in applause. Crutcher had given everyone a powerful reminder that, as artists, each of these young people has the ability to effect great change through their scholarship and artistry. For Crutcher, being a cellist is as important as being an academic, and he is convinced that the discipline he gained from practicing and playing has helped him on his journey.

One of the "rules" for prospective graduation speakers is that they teach a master class during the school year. This allows them to get to know the class and learn about students' aspirations and struggles so they can tailor their comments on the big day. Playwright and actress Melinda Lopez talked about growing up in an immigrant family and how her writing continues to focus on that feeling of being uprooted and searching for how to belong. She shared her struggle of becoming an artist when there was pressure from her family to have a more stable or lucrative career.

I believe that BAA, like many successful high schools, has created an environment where students, in part because they feel deeply that they belong and that their contributions are worthwhile, work hard to achieve their dreams. To some extent this happens through exposure to role models who are well integrated into the curriculum and daily life of the school. But even more importantly, students find success in school because it is a vibrant and responsive community with a positive school culture. This means being in a milieu that is free of judgment and embraces risk taking. It also means that there are clear expectations that adults and young people will demonstrate compassion and collaboration.

BAA works hard to build a strong sense of community that goes far beyond pep rallies and prom and to find ways for students to participate in the creation of that community. One way that communities become strong is through consistency of leadership and faculty. This allows for discussions over many years about what the community stands for and why. Another way is through the development of and commitment to a set of shared values.

One of our shared values, diversity with respect, is demonstrated best by Nancy. As a high school student, she reaped the benefits of being expected to give back to her community by developing the strong sense of agency that comes from making a difference in the lives of others. For her senior project, she developed a program that would bring music to an area in the Dominican Republic. She hoped that music would be a bridge between two cultures that were experiencing deep-seated animosity toward one another. Later as a college student, she further developed that project and received monetary support from her university to found a nonprofit, still in operation today. Now as a music teacher for students with severe learning disabilities, Nancy has continued to find ways to integrate music into the lives of individuals from underserved communities so that they can develop skills of self-advocacy and communication. Nancy's ability to make a difference in the world connects to her understanding of the importance of being known well—of belonging—and being part of a community where there are high expectations and support. She is also adamant that in a world filled with many perspectives, cultures, and languages, she has a responsibility to create greater empathy and understanding of differences. This is what she teaches and gives to her students every day.

Another of BAA's shared values is community with social responsibility. I will never forget when the entire junior class clasped hands to form a line of solidarity from the first floor computer lab to the third-floor office where the box to hand in Humanities 3 papers was located under the ominous sign "NO LATE PAPERS. 5PM DEADLINE." One student was having trouble with the printer and his paper was going to be late, but the students decided that if they made a human chain and passed in papers from the first floor all the way up to the third, one at a time, they would become one person and the late paper would just be part of the chain. I thought it was an ingenious move on the part of the students, and certainly demonstrated how they had internalized and interpreted this shared value. Cooperation is part of what our students learn. They pick each other up. They understand that together they are stronger than individually, and they care about their collective success.

There is an additional message that BAA imparts through the many guest speakers and artists who work with our students. Being an individual artist is not enough; you are also part of a community, and that community matters. Individual success can come from group solidarity. A third shared value, vision with integrity, acknowledges that others have paved the way for you and that humility is an important quality even in a cutthroat competitive world.

Over the years, world-famous musicians like Quincy Jones, nationally renowned visual artists such as Rick Lowe, and locally known artists and educators such as Beth Balliro, also a founding BAA teacher, have shared their work and stories with countless generations of BAA students. These artists recount, in their own words and actions, how they embody some of the same values BAA teaches.

When Quincy Jones taught a master class during school vacation week one year, we wondered if students would show up. They did. We'd been warned that the talk would be brief because his schedule was tight. Jones shared stories about his own tough upbringing and then discussed his commitment to social justice, civil rights, and health care. He talked about using one's celebrity to fight for what's right in the world. He also underscored his commitment, through the Quincy Jones Musiq Consortium, to teach the history of American music to young people throughout the country. At the end of his talk, which was over an hour long, everyone got a hug from him.

Visual artist Rick Lowe came to discuss his work as a painter and the founding of Project Row Houses in Houston, Texas. Project Row Houses is a neighborhood revitalization project that has stemmed gentrification in one of Houston's oldest African American neighborhoods. It has also brought youth education and even jobs to the area. Lowe emphasized the social role of art in neighborhood revitalization and explained how this project came from the vision and activism of local African American artists wanting a positive creative presence in their own community. Lowe reminded students that as artists they also have a responsibility to strengthen the communities from which they come, and his work embodies that ethos.

Beth Balliro, now a professor at Massachusetts College of Art and Design, talked about her work helping others on campus better understand the experiences of students of color and those who are their family's first generation to attend college. She discussed her commitment to developing art skills in more young people of color in urban schools, and the importance of continuing to discuss and confront the difficulties most Americans face in talking about race, white supremacy, and power. She shared some of the artwork that she had constructed with her students when asked about their experiences as people of color on a white-dominated campus. Both the videos and the commentary were riveting, and BAA students had an opportunity to think about how they too might do this kind of action research for their Senior Grant Project.[1]

Students could easily understand and see evidence of how these three artists used both celebrity and agency, as well as their artistry, to make changes in their communities—locally and internationally.

BAA's humanities curriculum begins with a simple question: "What is the role of an artist in society?" The curriculum design emphasized this three-pronged approach of scholarship, artistry, and community involvement. The last clarifies our meaning of "citizens." How are you a citizen of this world? What do you contribute and why? These are questions that could be asked of any student, in any school. The Senior Grant Project at BAA provides a long-term project so that students can answer those questions. In considering "what do I contribute?" one can see how "what I do matters"—a big part of believing in your own ability to make things happen, and your ability to make dreams a reality for yourself and others.

As part of the Senior Grant process, students are asked to describe the root causes of the issues that they, as artists, want to explore. This curriculum allows students to both formally and purposefully begin to define how their art can expose and illuminate an issue in the community. Students learn to have honest dialogues with stakeholders and do action research about the systemic obstacles in their communities. While their art can offer and inspire transformation and solutions, it is through careful research that students come to deeply understand an issue like homelessness among teens or how young people react to a parent's having been imprisoned. This ability to thoroughly comprehend an issue or a cause and to also think through ways to support that issue may translate into an ability to self-advocate in college or a career. Many BAA alumni talk about how their connection to the issue that they selected, starting in junior year in high school, has had positive repercussions throughout their lives.

Jessica tackled the question of teen homelessness and did action research with a variety of community agencies that supported teens. She even spent a long night on the street with teens to understand their predicament. This became a one-woman show, in the style of Anna Deavere Smith, that Jessica performed to raise funds for a youth program that worked with homeless teens. Another student, Miriam, created a short animated film that challenged "the lack of queer people in youth television," and pointed out that "young people of non-straight identities are censored in media, which pushes them to question where they fit in the current paradigm." In doing this project, which was helpful for so many other youth, Miriam came to realize that she felt a responsibility to share her ideas and her thinking. "And I know that this film helped me figure out some stuff that was really getting in my way too." Before doing the project, Miriam hadn't felt very engaged in school, but when school became where she could express herself, and where her teachers encouraged her to explore her ideas through film, her attitude and her grades both improved. "My teachers wouldn't let me create just an okay film. It had to be really good." Even though the assignment was a requirement for her Senior Grant Project, as well as a graduation requirement, it became much more important to Miriam than just checking off the boxes.

Across the country, several other programs have demonstrated the effectiveness of student action research in both empowering students and increasing academic outcomes. Ernest Morell and his colleagues document a project that occurred in Los Angeles with high school students from a variety of city schools. Along with adult mentors and chaperones, students in the Council of Youth Research engaged in action research about issues of concern to their lives and their experiences. One of their projects focused on inequities in student achievement outcomes (college-going rates) based on the foundation funding for various schools in different neighborhoods. In her field notes, one student compares the conditions of three schools:

> When my group went to Richside High School a teacher who gave us a tour of the school said that that school didn't have much either, comparing Richside to other inner city schools. But that school had a planetarium, three cafeterias, and a whole new science and technology building. While when my group went to my school South Central High, teachers complained about not having enough time to teach students because of furlough days and the ESL and Special Ed teachers don't have enough staff for all the students. And when my group went to Innercity High we saw how terrible the school's physical conditions were.[2]

Based on such observations, students argued that the way schools are funded creates more inequality in student outcomes. They began to see that schools in some more middle-class neighborhoods received more enrichment programs and better prepared teachers than those in poorer neighborhoods. As a result of their research, the students created presentations with their findings to various school and city officials in order to raise awareness and hopefully create changes in policies and funding formulas. Morell and other researchers argue, in the spirit of Paolo Freire's work, that when youth can own and name their world—or experience *conscientization*—they can begin to appropriate the tools of research and be prepared to make an impact on their own realities.[3]

In a very different vein, High School for Recording Arts in Minneapolis, geared to students who have been pushed out or are at risk of further marginalization by America's education system, uses the recording studio and particularly the arts and culture of hip hop to have students analyze, interpret, and then promote changes to their own reality. Students have recorded compositions that confront numerous issues in their own community such as police and community relations, climate change, seat belt awareness and promotion of healthy life styles through cycling. At this school, remix culture runs through the entire curriculum as students are taught and encouraged to be change agents.

At Social Justice High School in Chicago, all students complete a "Fire Project," which includes their personal philosophy of social justice, as well as what the research says.[4] Students have examined issues as varied as national debt, prostitution, shoe manufacturing, racial profiling, and lack of green space in their city. Students must complete multiple phases for project completion including action research, scholarly evidence, reflection, and presentation. The final paper includes an in-depth explanation of root causes as well as action steps and time lines that recommend short- and long-term solutions. Finally, students also present their findings in an eight to ten minute speech before a panel of teachers and community members (selected because of their expertise in the field represented by the topic). The goal at this school is that all students will have the skills as young researchers to create change in their world.

Whether in Chicago, Los Angeles, or Boston, these students experience the power of making an impact in their own communities, which solidifies their belief in themselves. Back at BAA, another alumna describes how during high school, everything she did was about creating change for those who would come after her. As a student, June was able to participate in a year-long internship that allowed her to deeply understand the issue of food justice. Her senior project was the culmination of that work. "I was willing to work really hard on the issue of school lunch because I knew that it wasn't just for me but for lots of generations, and then when I learned it was also about the wages that the kitchen workers made, that made it even more complicated. We weren't just talking about healthy food for students but also about who the people were that worked in the food service industry." June, now a teacher herself, continues, "Students need to know that school is more than just taking tests. I knew that my ideas and opinions were valued when I was a sophomore in high school. And that matters." BAA teaches students that they matter deeply—both to the role models that come into the school and to the faculty and staff. The students have a responsibility to use their artistry and scholarship to give back to one another and their communities. They are held to high expectations and given enormous support to meet those expectations. We see in the following stories of Diane and Carina how their sense of their own agency and the power of community helped them through many struggles. They also both reference the teachers and others whom they met who served as role models and mentors.

DIANE: IN THE COUNTRY WE LOVE

One of BAA's most famous alumni is Diane Guerrero, *Orange Is the New Black* and *Jane the Virgin* actress and author of the memoir *In the Country We Love: My Family Divided*. Diane, who graduated in 2004, is an artist-scholar-citizen extraordinaire. In her book, she tells the heartbreaking story of being a child of undocumented parents who were deported while she was in high school. Diane describes coming home from school and immediately sensing something was wrong. She had rushed home, eager to share with her parents the exciting news that her music teacher had asked her, then only a freshman, to sing a duet at the prestigious Springfest music concert. But the apartment was empty. Shortly thereafter a neighbor told Diane what had happened. Immigration officials had arrested her parents, who were undocumented. Although Diane had been born a citizen of the United States, she was now an unaccompanied minor. I remember sitting with her after she learned about her parents. The entire administrative team, as well as teachers, came together as a community and tried to figure out how she would be able to stay and finish high school with no family in Boston. We brainstormed various ways we could help Diane solve her very difficult situation, and we let her know that no matter what, we were there for her. She would be successful. We would make certain of that. And we knew Diane would do her part too.

"I was kinda shy when I got to BAA," she tells a crowded room of BAA students. On a book tour, she has returned for the first time to her alma mater, and the visit is an emotional one for her. "But I was still social, and I had a boyfriend the whole time in high school. There were lots of divas in the music department, but I didn't consider myself a diva. I was so excited by Springfest. It was the first time we were going to really show our stuff. Everyone's parents were coming. It was at Berklee [School of Music]. Really professional. I kept thinking maybe my parents would be there. They would have found a way back. My world kinda shattered all over again then." Diane's dark hair frames her face. Her eyes fill easily with tears when she thinks of that horrible moment so many years ago. "Of course, I see my parents now. I can travel back at least once a year. But then, it was awful. Everything I knew and loved was gone, in just one short moment."

Diane spoke of how important the BAA community had been in helping her to persevere and of the role the arts had played in helping her rebound. "I didn't want to leave high school. BAA was where I belonged. I wanted to be taken seriously, but I didn't know how to ask for that. I shut down after my parents left. But I did do different things: I did [*The*] *Laramie Project*. That's when I knew I wanted to act. Ms. Jones [music teacher] had me in Rhythm and Voice. I wanted to do more. I wanted to be noticed. Remember lunch time performances? I never was brave enough to do those—I wanted to, desperately! But I thought I only shone behind closed doors. I thought I'd be teased! And then there was senior recital. That's when I knew I shone. That's when I knew I could do it."

Later, after she had wowed the room full of high school students, I had the chance to talk and reflect with Diane about her years since BAA. The whole college-application process was a blur for her. "I knew I had to go because otherwise where was I going to live? But I didn't understand anything, really." She applied to a local four-year Catholic college and got full financial aid. She hoped college would give her a chance to focus and find something that was just "her." She did well in classes but was constantly distracted by the singing and theater she wasn't doing—so much so that she dropped out her senior year. "I had only two semesters to go, but I bombed," she said. "I had to return to my art."

Diane depicts the next few years of bouncing around trying to make ends meet, working as a paralegal and tending bar at night. She fit in an acting class here and there. One class led to some parts in student films and that led to a part in a small film being shot in Boston. The film did well, and she began to get noticed in Boston. She realized that she had to pursue "this acting thing" and that there wasn't enough work in Boston. She made the decision to move to New York City and live with an aunt, hoping for a lucky break. She got it with *Orange Is the New Black*. Playing Maritza Ramos on the series has opened many doors for this rising star, but she insists that her life as an artist is still unpredictable.

"I get kicked in the face every day," she says. "You have to be okay with auditioning all the time. And not getting the parts . . . You still have to get out there every day, and that's hard, especially when people are telling you that you aren't pretty enough, talented enough, and all that."

I hear the same Diane from high school—worrying about whether she was good enough and whether anyone would notice her. I am not sure Diane has to worry any more about being well known: she has recently won the SAG award for Best Latina actress, and her book, written with Michelle Burford of the Oprah Winfrey Network, is a success. Diane has told a story that millions of Americans experience, and she has told it well. Diane definitely has the limelight now, and she truly embodies the meaning of "If you believe, your dreams will come true." Like so many actors, she has to fight back those demons of vulnerability and lack of confidence every day, but as Diane has embraced the "citizen" part of being an artist-scholar-citizen, she has found a powerful and enduring way to use her art and her brilliance to improve the lives of others. As she has toured with her book, and told her own story, she has become a powerful spokesperson for immigration reform. She was named White House Ambassador for Citizenship and Naturalization in 2015, and she has worked with Immigration and Legal Resource Center and Mi Familia Vota, a nonpartisan Latino civic engagement organization, to promote citizenship and voter registration. Her book is being developed as a pilot TV drama that centers on a corporate attorney who starts taking pro bono cases for undocumented immigrants. For another pilot Diane is working on, she insisted on changing her character from Puerto Rican to Colombian American since "representing her community is very important to her."[5] Just this past month, Diane created a video in collaboration with Immigrant Legal Resource Center in which she reminds the general public that "we are all immigrants." Using her star power, Diane is ensuring that the world will listen to her. Certainly the current students at BAA listened to her—and were in awe. For many, Diane's story was their story too. One freshman told her teacher afterwards, "I have never felt so hopeful. If Diane can make it, so can I. I want to be as strong as she was and now I will be."

What was it that allowed Diane to overcome such great odds and achieve at this level? I think that being part of a vibrant and healthy high school community where both the individual and the collective were prized gave her a very strong sense that what she did—what she created—and who she was mattered to both the adults and to her peers. BAA's four shared values—passion with balance, diversity with respect, community with social responsibility, and vision with integrity—help students see the importance of both giving back to their community while excelling individually. Furthermore, these values also underscore the importance of creating work that is deeply felt, and doing one's work well—as an artist, a scholar, and a citizen.

CARINA: IF I PUT MY MIND TO SOMETHING, I'M GOING TO DO IT

Carina talks about how high school was an opportunity to live her dreams. "We had discussions in advisory about the steps we needed to take in order to get to college. In some ways the teachers really laid it out for us. And since we had all four grades in advisory, we could see what seniors wanted to achieve even when we were freshmen. They were like our role models. And we had lots of people coming and talking to us about different fields like engineering and acting. And some of those people looked like me."

She had decided she was going to be a Broadway actress. "I auditioned for everything at BAA. I loved acting, but I also loved building sets and hanging the lights." And Carina had a female teacher at BAA who worked professionally in technical theater, as a set designer. Even as a young student, Carina began to realize that technical fields were not "just for men" and that she loved solving difficult problems in set and lighting design, as well as in science and math classes. Carina had the chance to audition for a television program that was all about design and engineering. "Suddenly I was hanging around with so many smart kids talking about how their dad was an engineer, and how they liked inventing things," she said. Carina never thought she'd make it to the next round. "We had to work in teams of three to answer a challenge. I loved our challenge—to invent something that would make your bed in the morning." Carina had the idea of sewing magnets on the blankets so a robot hand could help make the bed. "I guess they liked my ideas because they called me at lunch on my job and offered me a position. That was a total 180 for me, just turned my life around." Carina ended up majoring in physics in college and has been working at an aerospace company for the past few years as an operations manager. She hopes to pursue a master's in engineering.

She talks about how her beliefs got her through. "If you are thinking it, your thoughts can become things." Given Carina's difficult entry to the US, and her eventual success in gaining asylum in her new country, she has learned that "if you believe it, you will do it." She remembers the harrowing experience of leaving her home country, El Salvador, and going to Mexico City. "It was a two-day ride from there to the US border. Then, we contacted the coyote. We met in a motel. There were about ten of us. My mom and I were the only girls. That day they gave us some food. And then we started walking through tunnel after tunnel. It's all dark. All you hear are drops of water." Carina described getting out of the darkness many, many hours later (Or was it days? She wasn't sure) and crossing a major street and hiding in the bushes until the coyote told them to run again. "You run; you hide and you do it again. I just remember being so hungry." Carina doesn't really know how her family was spared from capture by immigration officials, but they made it to New Jersey, where her grandmother was waiting for her. The family worked with immigration lawyers so that they could apply for asylum. At the same time, Carina was one of the lucky ones. She was given special amnesty, which meant she would be eligible for college scholarships at private universities.

"I always knew: I'm going to college. I heard that every day in high school. But graduating with a degree in physics—I'm proud of that. I don't know how I did it! I pray once in a while. I stay in touch with God. I pray before I eat and when I wake up, I just say, *Muchas gracias.* Thank you. . . . If I'm feeling down, I can turn to religion. I stick to that and it helps." Carina also described how she regularly called her high school advisor and math teacher all during college. She would sometimes come back to school for extra tutoring and support, and she always knew her high school teacher would give her help over the phone. "Lots of people believed in me. Lots of people gave me help, especially from my BAA community." She also talks about how she continues to reach out to help other immigrant youth. She knows the fear and worry that her family members experienced and she tries to find time to mentor young people in her neighborhood who may be undocumented. Now she is in the process of buying a house. She wants to be sure that her mother is comfortable. But she isn't losing sight of her dreams. "I want to do aeronautical engineering—crash engineering—and I have to go to graduate school for that. I will. I know it." BAA's strong sense of community supported Carina both during high school and after graduation. Furthermore, her exposure to so many different kinds of people doing a variety of jobs gave her a sense of how expansive her world could be.

HELPING OTHERS BELIEVE: ARTISTS AS ACTIVISTS

Many of my alumni who carved out their unique pathways give me enormous hope that we can make the necessary changes in this country's educational system to give the young people who come after them a more just future. Derrick, June, and Tory are just three examples of young people confronting the assumptions that have framed this book.

Derrick reflects on how his education prepared him to see himself as a change maker. "For me, BAA was a chance to really think about what it means to live in this free country. My family came as immigrants and we hadn't ever experienced a place where you weren't in constant danger that another group was going to take over and kill your family. That's what life was like back home." Even though Derrick was born in the United States, the stories of life in West Africa have been imbedded in his mind. "Here I could be anyone I wanted to be. I didn't have to worry. And at BAA we certainly could stand up for what we believed was right, even if others disagreed." Derrick described how difficult it was for him to come out as a gay man. "There was nothing in my family that prepared them for that. I know you [the teachers] were very supportive of me, but I wanted my parents to embrace me. That was just too hard for them." Derrick describes how he and his parents have an uneasy truce and a sort of "don't ask-don't tell" agreement. "I know there is a lot of love there but we won't talk about who I really am." Derrick is comfortable with his sexuality now, even though his parents may not be, but he is furious about the current political situation. "It's up to us to do something about the current regime. We learned about oppression and power in high school—and college too—and we will have to keep organizing and keep writing and keep making art that exposes these awful politicians. Some of us should move to Ohio or other Rust Belt states. We got too comfortable here." Derrick talks about how BAA consciously constructed curriculum that helped young people see artists and activists who looked like them. "We talked about 'artist-scholars-citizens' and where we were going to make an impact and how. And we met so many people that were doing just that." In particular Derrick talks about his classmate who interned at Company One Theater Company of Boston. "I saw a lot of the plays there—whether Chris [his friend] was cast or not—and the stories that Company One presents are a lot of what we have to think about in this country today. We need plays that tell the stories of gay people or other people who have experienced oppression. That's the only way we will make things better—by getting folks to realize what hurts and how to work together." Derrick like many other BAA graduates is also involved in politics. "We can't say just like Clinton did, 'America is great because America is good.' I think we say, 'America is great because *Americans* are good.' We need to communicate our lived experiences with one another with the intent of creating a national dialogue. There are systemic problems everywhere. Look, we started learning about this in high school. We all did senior projects. Now we have to work harder. It's our job to keep at it." Derrick says he will travel across the country taking pictures and videos that will allow him and others to understand race. "How do we think about race is this country? How can we stop being racist?" Derrick insists that his high school education was where he began to realize that he could use his artistry and scholarship to create and say something that would matter for people in this country.

June, the alum who worked on food justice issues and is now a teacher, knows about Derrick's work and applauds the fact that he will use his art to talk about race. She would like to create a similar experience for her students, but she describes how difficult it has been in her large, traditional, comprehensive high school. It's frustrating to know that the kind of learning involved to pass standardized tests does not bolster students' sense of agency or belonging, and there is little room for the kind of learning that would.

She tells me, "We say to our students, 'Social justice matters; the issues in your community, in your neighborhood matter—now finish writing the five-paragraph essay.'" Students know that their education, then, is not genuine. It's all about getting a score on a test—not tackling real problems that can make a difference in their lives today. Her students need opportunities to discuss how they are feeling about the recent national elections, or other issues facing their families and their lives like hunger and insecurity about their immigration status. However, she feels these discussions take a back seat to getting good grades and passing classes. "Sure, all that is important, but if we can't instill in our students a sense that their education is about community empowerment and change, what difference will it make in the long run?"

June deeply believes that schools can embrace those issues of concern to young people. "We can teach young people to do action research. That is a valid and important way to collect data and to think." June recalls a project she was involved with during intersession at BAA, when she and her peers visited a variety of different schools (charter, district, exam, etc.) to see how students described the education they were getting. "We were interested in whether students had a sense of their own agency in their schools. Did they feel that school was connected to their lives? Did they think about whether their ideas mattered at school?" That project cemented June's belief that schools needed to be places where students deeply feel that they can make change. As a teacher today, June feels it's urgent for traditional schools to think more broadly about what they want to accomplish with young people. "The way we are doing it now isn't working."

June is right. Teaching to the test is demoralizing and will not create an ethos of students believing in their ability to effect change for their own lives and those of others. Nor will schools be able to create communities that value ongoing conversations and commitments to equity and engagement of students in the learning process. Just as BAA has a commitment to view our students as artists within a larger community, all schools need to find ways to embrace their students as members of a community that matters—whether organized around social justice, leadership, health, or being the next group of IT managers.

Students are curious about the issues that have shaped their communities, and they need opportunities to explore those histories. Students want to understand why things operate the way they do—whether from a mathematical, or economic or humanistic perspective. When schools are set up to provide opportunities for students to probe those questions, students are more apt to engage in finding answers that can positively shape their own futures and make change for a better world.

One of my alums is working to make that change. Tory, a local actor and playwright, has just released a video explaining his Kamikazee Art project. He describes it as a "crisis response team made of artists." In the video, Tory talks about how the world is crazy and becoming crazier, but as an artist, he knows how to filter anger and use it toward something good. Tory aims to make art that will connect people across differences. His work is a response to the recent spate of horrific shootings of unarmed black men across the nation as well as the mass shootings in a South Carolina church and an Orlando club. He writes, "When tragedies hit our world, country, or town, instead of just being angry and posting about it, [on Facebook] Kamikazee gives you the chance to convert that anger into inspiration and awareness. With the use of pop up events, we will give the public a chance to deal with their grief, anger, and frustration through creativity. We are at war with hatred, bigotry, and prejudice. They have their army. It's time we have ours. An army of art Kamikazes with unwavering commitment to disrupt the status quo, going into the battlefield armed with paint, paper, and each other."

Tory signs off, "Love People, Make Art." He is telling his story and making sure that we join him. For me, Tory exemplifies the highest aims of education: belief in yourself and your own dreams but also in the collective dreams of social justice and equity.

TO SOAR AND TO DREAM

Some students dream it and do it. Diane's SAG Award is likely just the beginning for her. She has spoken and written about the traumas she experienced in high school when her parents were deported, but she never stopped believing in her abilities to reach her dreams, and she relied on her high school community to support her. She has become a powerful spokesperson for immigration reform. Carina, now an engineer, continued to rely on her BAA community so that she didn't give up. During college, her high school teachers continued to tutor her and shared her dream that she could accomplish whatever she set her mind to. Kirven, Derrick, and June were also positively shaped by their high school experiences. I tell these stories in celebration of all that can be accomplished when young people are given the tools to soar and to dream. These young people believed in themselves and saw that their contributions to a community were valued.

Many others whom I taught have also dreamed it, but they couldn't do it. We could conclude that they didn't "have what it takes" or that they didn't work hard enough, didn't believe strongly enough. In some cases, these conclusions may be true and may be responsible for some of the student's difficulty. But we have to recognize that more than dreaming and follow-through are involved. Rather than looking to grit as the answer, we have to change structures to make the obstacles less daunting. We can't adopt a Social Darwinist attitude and conclude that those who are strong enough will make it. Some who are just as determined will, for reasons beyond their control, be unable to get that lucky break.

Structural inequities and chance notwithstanding, schools still can give a good foundation in the skills needed to tackle complex issues. Projects like BAA's Senior Grant challenge students to analyze a problem and develop a feasible solution. Thus, the higher-level skills of research, analysis, creative thinking, problem-solving, and persistence all become part of the curriculum. And, more importantly, some students will actually implement their projects. I would like to see more students, whether as eighth or twelfth graders, be able to carry out such a plan as part of their capstone experiences. By doing so, I believe students will develop a sense of self-worth and agency that will help them surmount systemic obstacles.

School can be the place where you practice how dreams are realized. School can be where you can build a strong sense of self—an identity that you belong to a special tribe, like artists, or change-makers, or mathematicians or inventors. To ensure that schools incubate future dreams and dreamers, curriculum, structures, and pedagogy must encourage deep engagement both with teachers and with community members. The walls between school and community can and should be permeable.

This belief that you can make a difference in your community need not exist only in arts schools. Certainly all schools can develop curriculum that relate to students' role as scholars-citizens. I have worked with many other schools that start with an essential question such as "What does it mean to be an American?" or "Who built America?" These kinds of questions allow for sustained exploration that can deeply engage students in their own learning. When students feel invested and inspired in their school they will tackle seemingly insurmountable problems that make education worthwhile.

Just the other day, I saw this play out in a unique way at a local elementary school. I sat in on a board meeting at the Mission Hill School, a pilot public elementary school in Boston. There were nearly fifty people in the room, all debating the issues of the day. The agenda involved voting on the budget and how to deal with the fact that many families opted out of high-stakes testing. These were both heady topics, but the topic that many students wanted to discuss (at Mission Hill, students are represented on the board and have an equal vote to parents and teachers) was the issue of whether seventh graders should be allowed to wear headphones in order to listen to music while doing quiet work in class. This was clearly a controversial subject, and the seventh-grade student was having a hard time making his case to teachers and parents. Finally, a younger student, maybe a fifth grader, spoke up. Quietly he said, "I think actions should speak louder than words, and we, as a school, should give the seventh graders the chance to prove that they can do this responsibly. I propose we vote for this." The motion passed. These young people have been given an important opportunity to construct their own community and take responsibility for it.

Belief in yourself is built through seeing that your contributions to a community are valued, and that your actions have an impact. Diane and certainly Carina both experienced a supportive community. Students like Derrick and June also felt empowered to make contributions to the larger community, in large part because of the collaborative structures in place at BAA. I am particularly proud of the ways that my alums have become change agents well beyond high school. And I am encouraged by the use of participatory action research and capstone projects in many schools across the country.

The triumphant stories told here give us reason to celebrate. They are, of course, the reason I am still in education. I want to ensure the success of another generation of young people. These students are our pride and joy; they dreamed it and they did it. We need to find ways for more schools to create communities for dreamers and doers.

CONCLUSION

I began this book by reflecting on the promise that I had made to my freshmen during the fourteen years I was headmaster of Boston Arts Academy: "All of you will graduate from high school and go on to college or a career." Over the years, hearing the stories of many alumni, I began to feel uneasy about the promise I had been making. On the one hand, nearly two-thirds have graduated from college, which is way above the national norm for urban schools. On the other hand, what about the remaining one-third, whose aspirations of a college degree or solid career had been thwarted? And even for those who *have* graduated, what about the toll their journey had taken on them? My students' stories illustrated that many of the assumptions that guide public education and higher education discourse are simply not valid.

We assume that all students start in the same place, that everyone has access to the same degree of knowledge necessary to navigate the college years. A recent *New York Times* article described this problem: "For young people with college-educated parents, the path to higher education may be stressful, but there is a road map. If their standardized test scores are too low, they can pay for a prep course; if their essay is lackluster, they can hire a writing coach. No one will be the wiser. If they can't decide which college is the 'best fit,' they can visit. When they are tempted to give up, their parents will push them on."[1] However, few of these supports are in place for low-income or first-generation students.

We assume that deep social inequities can be overcome by individual effort, that everyone has an equal chance of success. We assume that those who are "making it" prove that anyone can make it, and those who are not successful have only themselves to blame. These assumptions benefit the few over the many, and when they go unchallenged, our society becomes ever more fractured and unequal. The assumptions Americans make about low-income black and brown students in urban settings are often tied to bedrock myths about how this nation works (fairly and equitably), and who those kids are and what they need. Sometimes we believe "those kids" need punitive and remedial support—because we see them as *not the same* as white middle-class students. Yet, at other times, our educational system prefers to see them as *the same*, and ignores that they may need additional resources, guidance counselors, financial assistance, and so on. Systemic issues have created nearly insurmountable barriers for my students. I want to ensure that their successes are seen against this backdrop of inequity so that we can stop idealizing these stories and, instead, consider the cost of success.

The other day Peter, a BAA alum, came to see me and we discussed the assumptions that frame this book. He said, "Yeah, I think all of those assumptions affected me—and not all in a good way. I'm finally getting my degree. It's taken me almost fifteen years. Lots of loans and lots of part-time jobs. Lots of leaving school and coming back. And I'm one of the lucky ones. I'm going to be a music teacher. Eventually. Finally. All this talk of grit—I don't think that's good for kids, really. I want to teach compassion and love, and the importance of dignity. I almost lost mine. I know I have something to offer young people. I want them to find their passion just like you all did for me so many years ago, but I don't want it to take others so long."

I am committed to creating a world in which Peter's journey is not so difficult. Through interviews and informal discussions with over eighty alums, and through research and interviews with other experts, I began to develop a deeper inquiry: *In the face of such ongoing inequality, how does one (or leaders collectively) respond in an ethical way?* And even more broadly, what needs to change in both pre-K–12 education and in higher education so that our promises are consistent with students' reality? I believe that some of what I have discussed in these chapters provides a way forward. We must commit to antiracist education in our classrooms and colleges; we must reinvest in career and technical education at all levels; we need better articulated support systems for first-generation college students and national policies that make college-going (and graduating) affordable. In sum, we need to recommit to a more equitable vision of education. Previous policies have failed to accomplish these goals.

This country's current obsession with high-stakes testing has nearly obliterated what I consider to be the most important purposes for schooling:

- helping students understand the context of their lives
- empowering students to create social change and solve problems that will improve living conditions and increase well-being
- teaching students to embrace differences and to get along with others
- providing skill development, as well as opportunities for joy, beauty, play, and playfulness

Schools have multiple and sometimes competing purposes. School is, of course, about skill attainment and filling the jobs our country needs, but school must also be about learning to get along with and listen to one another—across a wide range of differences. School is where we develop understanding of our history and how to live and participate in our society. School is where we learn how to advance our democracy. School is where we can be exposed to ideas that will lead to jobs and opportunities that don't even exist yet. I have argued throughout this book that school needs to be where we practice and realize our individual and collective dreams.

I have also argued for a vision of education that embraces arts and creativity. Schools need to be wary of rigid behavioral systems that value compliance above all else. While no one believes in chaos in schools, we must be critical of how far some schools and educators have gone in the "taming" of black and brown children. The dominant discussions today are about test scores and teaching for grit. No one ranks or sorts schools based on how much music or art students study. And few research projects are being funded that ask whether students have more advanced executive-functioning skills because they play music together. (The few studies out there demonstrate positive correlations.) We need a reinvestment in the primary role of arts, music, and creativity in our schools. I have argued before that one of the most powerful ways of helping young people (and adults) understand and value differences is through the arts. When we can sing in another language, dance a story that is foreign to us, or learn poetry from a culture we are unfamiliar with, we have the opportunity to grow as more self-aware individuals. School needs to be a place where individual students can feel their whole self is welcome and valued—meaning their culture, language, gender, sexual orientation, race, and ethnicity. And we need teachers and leaders who know how to embrace those wonderfully varied individuals.

My work now focuses on leadership development. I hope the next generation of leaders can create schools that address the hard questions I have raised here. I am emboldened by the work of an emerging leader who is dedicated to bringing antiracist education to her middle school students and faculty, despite resistance. Natalia describes the skepticism she met: "Some of my teachers actually said to me, 'Why are we doing all this culturally responsive teaching? I learned multicultural education in the eighties. I know how to deal with differences.'" Natalia describes her leadership efforts as an uphill battle, but one she is prepared for. "My job," she said, "is to make sure that the faculty realizes that antiracist work is a daily journey, not a one-shot thing. It's not something we do on Tuesday and then racism is gone." Natalia knows that her work is about equity and creating schools that can respond to all students in more ethical ways. She underscores that school *is* about learning about differences.

Kendra, whom we met in chapter 2, as she dealt with being one of only eleven students of color on her campus, knows something about differences. Kendra now works in the office of student affairs at an elite private college. "I guess after all my experiences as a young woman of color on a white campus, I knew this was an area in which I could help others," Kendra said. Tiana, a freshman in college, came to see Kendra during the exam period. Tiana was feeling very discouraged and Kendra tried to buoy her spirits and let her know that first semester is hard for everyone. They talked about her study habits and whether she was accessing supports such as the tutoring and writing center. But after a few minutes of discussion, it was clear that the issue wasn't about exams or studying. Kendra didn't want to pry too much but she finally decided to ask, "What's really bothering you?" Tiana's eyes welled up as she proceeded to tell Kendra about how everyone in her dorm received care packages from their parents to get them through the stress of studying and exams. "You know, cookies and teas and lotions and de-stressing stuff like that." Kendra listened quietly, remembering the exact same situation from her own experience as a student. Tiana continued, "And it's not that I need any of these things. And I feel badly for even feeling sad. I mean, I know what a sacrifice it is for my mom that I am here." Kendra nodded. "And your mom wouldn't even know about parents sending care packages, right?" she asked. Tiana looked up. "Right. And that's what makes me both sad and guilty at the same time. I want her to know, but I could never tell her. I wouldn't want her to feel badly after everything she's done." Tiana sighed, then continued. "I'm working hard here—so hard—my classes are great, and I know I'm getting a great education, and so I feel silly getting upset about these little things. But they just remind me how little I fit in." Kendra got up from her desk and gave Tiana a big hug. "Let's make a deal. When those care packages arrive, you just come and see me. I'll always have something special for you." The young woman smiled at Kendra and thanked her for being there for her. "Like I said, it's not about the stuff. I just needed to tell someone who would understand. I know it's silly."

But Kendra knows it's not silly. She understands from firsthand experience the weight and symbolism of that care package—of coming from a family of means and a tradition of college-going. She understands intimately Tiana's isolation. Kendra knows that the differences in race and privilege can keep students in separate spheres. She and her college employers know the importance that diversity in staffing makes to the many first-generation college students on her campus.

Kendra gives me hope, as does Natalia, that a more ethical vision of school is actually possible in this country. Both of these young women are poised to be part of the next generation of educational leaders who deeply understand the dangers of unexamined assumptions. They and others like them will move us forward to a more equitable future.

ACKNOWLEDGMENTS

Thank you to the many Boston Arts Academy alumni who shared their stories with me. Your successes and challenges have inspired this book. In a few instances I have used your real names, but in most cases I have obscured your identities. I hope that I have been respectful throughout this process. I am honored to have served as your principal.

I am very grateful to the many other individuals who were willing to be interviewed for this book. Whether you were an educator, a non-profit leader, a college administrator, professor, or a college president, your insights and experiences guided my thinking.

The Boston Arts Academy faculty and leadership, both current and former, shared their perspectives, experiences, and stories. The Boston Arts Academy board of trustees, of which I am now a proud member, offered support and encouragement throughout this project.

Many individuals read various versions of these chapters and gave helpful feedback and editing. My former graduate students—Richard Fournier, Tom McDermott, Alice Liou, and Michael Lipset—were wonderful editors. Anne Clark, Cynthia Hairston, Charlie Lyons, Ann Moritz, David Rosenberg, Eileen Shakespear, and Carmen Torres all provided valuable feedback. Maha Chourafa always provided the data I needed and talked me through definitions! Stephen Sun gave wonderful design ideas and advice.

Carmen, you have been part of many of these experiences. It is a privilege to work alongside you. Thank you for decades of friendship.

Benji, you read almost every word and set me straight when I was veering off track. Your clarity of thought has been invaluable to me throughout this process. It has been a source of enormous pride to be critiqued and challenged by my son!

Abbie, thank you for many discussions and shared experiences that found their way into these pages.

Sam, Amina, and, especially, Sana, you have been my motivation and inspiration.

Steve, your encouragement, patience, and good sense have helped at every stage of the writing process. I so appreciate your willingness to read, without groaning, yet another draft, and to talk with me about another possible idea or argument. Thank you for always reminding me to only write what I know.

Janie, your careful coaching got me through writing this book. You always challenge my ideas and make them better. I am so grateful for the many hours of editing and all the conversations. I can't wait to begin our work!

Jean and David Nathan, you were my first teachers.

Vito Perrone, Ted Sizer, and the work of the Coalition of Essential Schools all influenced my formation as an educator. Vito guided me through two decades of leading schools and learning to write about them. I am honored to codirect the Perrone-Sizer Institute for Creative Leadership in their names.

Alexis Rizzuto, I'm so glad I was on this journey with you. There is no better editor than you. Thank you for always steering me in the right direction and listening so well.

Thank you to my colleagues at Beacon Press—Rachael Marks, editor; Susan Lumenello, managing editor; and Melissa Dobson, copy editor, as well as the rest of the staff who had a hand in helping me with this book.

NOTES

INTRODUCTION: THE PROMISE

1. Boston Arts Academy, School and District Profiles, Massachusetts Department of Elementary and Secondary Education, http://profiles.doe.mass.edu /reportcard/rc.aspx?linkid=37&orgcode=00350546&fycode=2016&orgtype code=6, accessed May 10, 2017.

2. In 2015, the federal government changed "free and reduced lunch" to "economically disadvantaged." See *A Changing Metric: Low Income vs. Economically Disadvantaged* (Massachusetts Department of Elementary and Secondary Education, revised July 6, 2015).

3. Denisa R. Superville, "Graduation Rates Rise; Gap Between Black and White Males Grows, Report Says," *District Dossier* (blog), *Education Week*, February 11, 2015, http://blogs.edweek.org/edweek/District_Dossier/2015/02/as _nation_graduation_rate_grew.html; Nikhil Swaminathan, "Is Public Education Failing Black Male Students?" *Daily Good*, August 19, 2010, https://www.good.is /articles/is-public-education-failing-black-male-students; *Governing the States and Localities,* "High School Graduation Rates by State" (n.d.), http://www.governing .com/gov-data/high-school-graduation-rates-by-state.html.

4. School and District Profiles, Massachusetts Department of Elementary and Secondary Education, http://profiles.doe.mass.edu/, accessed May 2, 2017.

5. William C. Symonds, Robert Schwartz, and Ronald F. Ferguson, *Pathways to Prosperity: Meeting the Challenge of Preparing Young Americans for the 21st Century* (Cambridge, MA: Pathways to Prosperity Project, Harvard University Graduate School of Education, 2011).

6. Barry Bluestone and Alan Clayton-Matthews, *Life Sciences Innovation as a Catalyst for Economic Development: The Role of the Massachusetts Life Sciences Center* (Boston: Dukakis Center for Urban and Regional Policy, Northeastern University, 2013).

7. Barry Bluestone, *Staying Power II: A Report Card on Manufacturing in Massachusetts* (Boston: Dukakis Center for Urban and Regional Policy, Northeastern University, 2003).

8. Anthony P. Carnevale, Nicole Smith, and Jeff Strohl, *Recovery: Job Growth and Education Requirements Through 2020* (Boston: Georgetown Public Policy Institute, 2014), https://cew.georgetown.edu/wp-content/uploads/2014/11 /Recovery2020.ES_.Web_.pdf.

9. Diane Guerrero, *In the Country We Love* (New York: Henry Holt, 2016).

CHAPTER ONE: "MONEY DOESN'T HAVE TO BE AN OBSTACLE"

1. School and District Profiles, Boston Arts Academy, "2013-14 Graduates Attending Institutions of Higher Education: All Colleges and Universities," Massachusetts Department of Elementary and Secondary Education, http://profiles .doe.mass.edu/nsc/gradsattendingcollege_dist.aspx?orgcode=00350546&fycode =2015&orgtypecode=6&; Maha Chourafa, dean of educational planning, Boston Arts Academy, author interview, various dates. More information on graduation rates and persistence rates can be found at Andrew Sum et al., *Getting to the Finish Line: College Enrollment and Graduation; a Seven Year Longitudinal Study of the Boston Public Schools Class of 2000* (Boston: Center for Labor Market Studies, Northeastern University, 2008/2013), http://www.tbf.org/news-and-events/news /2013/january/~/media/TBFOrg/Files/Reports/PIC%20Report.pdf; and Michael Levenson, "College Graduation Rates for Boston Students Are Up, but That's Not the Whole Picture," *Boston Globe*, June 14, 2016, https://www.boston globe.com/metro/2016/06/14/college-graduation-rates-improve-for-boston -students-but-gaps-remain/4gC9MOioIpUP9i6RzOYPXN/story.html.

2. David L. Kirp, "What Can Stop Kids from Dropping Out," *New York Times*, April 30, 2016, https://www.nytimes.com/2016/05/01/opinion/sunday/what-can -stop-kids-from-dropping-out.html.

3. David Leonhardt, "America's Great Working-Class Colleges," *New York Times*, January 18, 2017, https://www.nytimes.com/2017/01/18/opinion/sunday /americas-great-working-class-colleges.html?_r=0.

4. Raj Chetty et al., "Mobility Report Cards: The Role of Colleges in Intergenerational Mobility, Equality of Opportunity Project," January 2017, http:// www.equality-of-opportunity.org/papers/coll_mrc_paper.pdf.

5. Christopher J. Nellum and Terry W. Hartle, "Where Have All the Low-Income Students Gone?," *Presidency* 19, no. 1 (Winter 2015).

6. "Tuition and Fees," Undergraduate Admissions, website of the University of Massachusetts–Amherst, https://www.umass.edu/admissions/facts-and-figures /tuition-and-fees, accessed May 2, 2017.

7. Joseph Stiglitz, "Student Debt and the Crushing of the American Dream," *New York Times,* May 13, 2013. For further reading on the financial aid system and student debt crisis, see Sara Goldrick-Rab, *Paying the Price: College Costs, Financial Aid, and the Betrayal of the American Dream* (Chicago: University of Chicago Press, 2016).

8. Maggie McGrath, "Money Isn't Everything: When It's Worth Taking On $50,000 or More in Student Debt," *Forbes*, April 4, 2014.

9. Gates Foundation Scholarships are some of the most competitive scholarships that students of color can apply for, and each year at BAA, we had a couple of students vying for one.

10. Neil Swidey, "Colleges Must Stop Holding Student Transcripts Hostage," *Boston Globe Magazine*, June 17, 2016, https://www.bostonglobe.com/magazine /2016/06/17/one-simple-way-colleges-should-help-students-debt-right-now /koNot1ccYhgA3qSYJBpFqK/story.html.

11. Bureau of Labor Statistics, "Education Still Pays," September 2014, http://www.bls.gov/careeroutlook/2014/data-on-display/education-still-pays.htm.

12. Neil Swidey, "The College Debt Crisis Is Even Worse Than You Think," *Boston Globe Magazine*, May 2016, https://www.bostonglobe.com/magazine/2016/05/18/hopes-dreams-debt/fR6ocKakwUlGokojTlONTN/story.html.

13. Eric Westervelt, "'I'm A Student-Debt Slave': How'd We Get Here?," *NPREd*, National Public Radio, July 11, 2016, http://www.npr.org/sections/ed/2016/07/11/484364476/im-a-student-debt-slave-howd-we-get-here.

14. There is another reason that students like Kevin attending UMass Dartmouth and other non-flagship state schools struggle, and that is because of huge discrepancies in how federal dollars and grants do or do not reach colleges with the most vulnerable populations. Consider this study by Richard Vedder, as reported by John Cassidy in the *New Yorker*. Vedder found that "in 2010 Princeton [University], which had an endowment of close to fifteen billion dollars, received state and federal benefits equivalent to roughly fifty thousand dollars per student, whereas the nearby College of New Jersey got benefits of two thousand dollars per student." While there is no equivalent study about UMass–Dartmouth and Harvard University, the same differences hold true. Of course, there may be valid reasons for rewarding excellence and sponsoring institutions that do important scientific research. But, as Cassidy asks, "Is a twenty-five-to-one difference in government support really justified?" These de facto policies further penalize students like Kevin. John Cassidy, "College Calculus," *New Yorker,* September 7, 2015, http://www.newyorker.com/magazine/2015/09/07/college-calculus.

15. Commission on the Future of Undergraduate Education, *A Primer on the College Student Journey* (Cambridge, MA: American Academy of Arts and Sciences, 2016).

16. Cassidy, "College Calculus."

17. Ibid., 8.

18. National Education Longitudinal Study of 2002, https://nces.ed.gov/surveys/els2002/, accessed May 2, 2017.

19. William G. Bowen, Matthew Chingos, and Michael S. McPherson, *Crossing the Finish Line: Completing College at America's Public Universities* (Princeton, NJ: Princeton University Press, 2011).

20. Carlos Santiago, Massachusetts commissioner of higher education, author interview, July 2016.

21. Pam Eddinger, president of Bunker Hill Community College, author interview, January 2017.

22. Laura Krantz, "College Placement Exam Comes Under New Scrutiny," *Boston Globe*, August 8, 2015, https://www.bostonglobe.com/metro/2015/08/07/college-placement-test-comes-under-scrutiny/30OEdpY54TFNSBkxhlF2EM/story.html.

23. Paul Fain, "Finding a New Compass," *Inside Higher Ed*, June 18, 2015, https://www.insidehighered.com/news/2015/06/18/act-drops-popular-compass-placement-test-acknowledging-its-predictive-limits.

24. "Transforming Developmental Math Education," Massachusetts Department of Higher Education, http://www.mass.edu/strategic/comp_developmath .asp, accessed May 22, 2017.

25. College for America, http://collegeforamerica.org/for-students/, accessed May 2, 2017.

26. Match Beyond website, http://www.matchbeyond.org/news/, accessed May 2, 2017.

27. Swidey, "The College Debt Crisis Is Even Worse Than You Think"; Doug Lederman, "For-Profit College Sector Continues to Shrink," *Inside Higher Ed*, July 15, 2016, https://www.insidehighered.com/quicktakes/2016/07/15/profit-college -sector-continues-shrink; Michael Stratford, "Pointing a Finger at For-Profits," *Inside Higher Ed*, September 11, 2015, https://www.insidehighered.com/news/2015/09/11 /study-finds-profit-colleges-drove-spike-student-loan-defaults; Shahien Nasiripour, "Many For-Profit College Graduates Earn Less Than Minimum Wage," *Bloomberg*, November 17, 2016, https://www.bloomberg.com/news/articles/2016-11-17/many-for -profit-college-graduates-earn-less-than-minimum-wage; Gillian B. White, "The Empty Promises of For-Profit Colleges," *Atlantic*, September 15, 2015, https://www.the atlantic.com/business/archive/2015/09/the-failure-of-for-profit-colleges/405301/.

28. Kathryn Vasel and Katie Lobosco, "For-Profit College ITT Shuts Down: Tens of Thousands of Students in the Lurch," *CNN Money*, http://money.cnn .com/2016/09/06/pf/college/itt-shuts-down/; Note, "Forgive and Forget: Bankruptcy Reform in the Context of For-Profit Colleges," *Harvard Law Review* 128 (May 9, 2015); 2018, https://harvardlawreview.org/2015/05/forgive-and-forget -bankruptcy-reform-in-the-context-of-for-profit-colleges/.

29. Anya Kamenetz, "Corinthian Colleges Misled Students on Job Placement, Investigation Finds," *NPREd* (blog), November 17, 2015, http://www.npr.org /sections/ed/2015/11/17/456367152/corinthian-misled-students-on-job-placement -investigation-finds.

30. Vasel and Lobosco, "For-Profit College ITT Shuts Down."

31. Quoted in James Surowiecki, "The Rise and Fall of For-Profit Schools," *New Yorker*, November 2, 2015, 34.

32. D. Radwin, J. Wine, P. Siegel, and M. Bryan, *2011–12 National Postsecondary Student Aid Study (NPSAS: 12): Student Financial Aid Estimates for 2011–12* (NCES 2013-165) (Washington, DC: National Center for Education Statistics, 2013), accessed March 21, 2017.

33. Stiglitz, "Student Debt and the Crushing of the American Dream."

34. "Predator Colleges May Thrive Again," *New York Times*, March 23, 2017, https://www.nytimes.com/2017/03/23/opinion/predator-colleges-may-thrive -again.html.

CHAPTER TWO: "RACE DOESN'T MATTER"

1. Terris Ross et al., *Higher Education: Gaps in Access and Persistence Study* (Washington, DC: National Center for Education Statistics, 2012), table 37-1, https://nces.ed.gov/pubs2012/2012046.pdf.

2. Debbie Bial, author interview, October 2015.

3. David Scharfenberg, "Boundaries to Hope," *Boston Globe*, September 2, 2016, https://www.bostonglobe.com/metro/2016/09/02/boundaries-hope/m15ni02 g8atfGwg4R9z7cI/story.html.

4. James Banks, *Multicultural Education: Issues and Perspectives* (Hoboken, NJ: John Wiley & Sons, 2009); Gilberto Conchas and James Diego Vigil, *Street Smart, School Smart: Urban Poverty and the Education of Adolescent Boys* (New York: Teachers College Press, 2012).

5. Glenn E. Singleton and Curtis W. Linton, eds., *Courageous Conversations: A Field Guide for Achieving Equity in Schools* (Thousand Oaks, CA: Corwin Press, 2005), 45.

6. Ibid.

7. Carmen Torres, former associate headmaster and then coheadmaster of Boston Arts Academy, was my cofacilitator for many of these workshops. Having the perspective of Torres, a person of color whose experiences are so different from my own, was crucial in ensuring that this diverse group of educators earned our trust and that of one another. It is critical for younger educators to see that veteran educators can work closely together across racial, language of origin, and social-class differences.

8. "Illustrating Equality vs. Equity" can be viewed at the website of Interaction Institute for Social Change, http://interactioninstitute.org/illustrating-equality -vs-equity/. For a provocative analysis of the illustration, see Paul Kuttner's blog *Cultural Organizing*, http://culturalorganizing.org/the-problem-with-that-equity -vs-equality-graphic/.

9. Peggy McIntosh, "White Privilege: Unpacking the Invisible Knapsack," *Peace and Freedom Magazine* (July/August 1989): 10–12, published by Women's International League for Peace and Freedom, Philadelphia.

10. "Cracking the Codes: Joy DeGruy, A Trip to the Grocery Store," YouTube, https://www.youtube.com/watch?v=Wf9QBnPK6Yg, uploaded September 20, 2011.

CHAPTER THREE: "JUST WORK HARDER"

1. For information on the Efficacy Institution, see http://www.efficacy.org.

2. Paul Tough, *How Children Succeed: Grit, Curiosity, and the Hidden Power of Character* (Boston: Houghton Mifflin Harcourt, 2012).

3. Deborah Perkins-Gough, "The Significance of Grit: A Conversation with Angela Lee Duckworth," *Educational Leadership* 71 (September 2013): 14–20.

4. Corey Donahue, "Helping Students Succeed by Building Grit," Carnegie Foundation for the Advancement of Teaching, *Carnegie Commons Blog*, https:// www.carnegiefoundation.org/blog/helping-students-succeed-by-building-grit/.

5. Jay Mathews, *Work Hard. Be Nice: How Two Inspired Teachers Created the Most Inspiring Schools in America* (Chapel Hill, NC: Algonquin, 2009).

6. In 2011, Wendy Kopp spoke on a Seattle radio station, saying that people often misunderstand the function of TFA. "We're a leadership-development organization, not a teaching organization," she said. "I think if you don't understand that, of course it's easy to tear the whole thing apart." See Alexandra Hootnick,

"Teachers Are Losing Their Jobs, but Teach for America's Expanding. What's Wrong with That?," *Hechinger Report*, April 21, 2014, http://hechingerreport.org/content /teachers-losing-jobs-teach-americas-expanding-whats-wrong_15617/.

7. "Grit Scale," http://angeladuckworth.com/grit-scale/.

8. Duckworth's work grew from the work of Dr. K. Anders Ericsson, who studied deliberate practice in areas such as chess, soccer, and music. Ericsson described successful deliberate practice as having four components: (1) setting a stretch goal; (2) fully concentrating on a single task; (3) receiving immediate and informative feedback; and (4) repetitive practice until fluent. See K. Anders Ericcson, Ralf Th. Krampe, and Clemens Tesch-Römer, "The Role of Deliberate Practice in the Execution of Expert Performance," *Psychological Review* 100, no. 3 (1993): 363–406, available at the website of the University of Southern California, Institute for Creative Technologies, http://projects.ict.usc.edu/itw/gel/EricssonDeliberatePracticePR93.PDF.

9. Tough, *How Children Succeed*, 89.

10. See Zaretta L. Hammond, *Culturally Responsive Teaching and the Brain: Promoting Authentic Engagement and Rigor Among Culturally and Linguistically Diverse Students* (Thousand Oaks, CA: Corwin Press, 2015).

11. Alice Liou, "Deconstructing the Oppression of Charter School Students: A Critical Race Theory Analysis of No-Excuses Schools," unpublished ms., 2016.

12. Kristina Rizga, "What White Teachers Can Learn from Black Preachers," *Mother Jones,* April 26, 2016, http://www.motherjones.com/print/302686.

13. Valerie Strauss, "Why 'No Excuses' Charter Schools Mold 'Very Submissive' Students—Starting in Kindergarten," *Washington Post*, September 19, 2014, https://www.washingtonpost.com/news/answer-sheet/wp/2014/09/19/why-no -excuses-charter-schools-mold-very-submissive-students-starting-in-kindergarten /?utm_term=.3b36a248bc51.

14. *Mathematica Research on KIPP Schools*, 2010 report, http://www.kipp .org/results/independent-reports/#mathematica-2010-report.

15. Panel discussion, National Time and Learning Conference, Boston, April 2008.

16. Wayne K. Hoy, C. John Tarter, and Anita Woolfolk Hoy, "Academic Optimism of Schools: A Force for Student Achievement," *American Educational Research Journal* 43, no. 3 (2006): 425–46.

17. *Noam Chomsky Quotes*, http://noam-chomsky.tumblr.com/post/6255757090 /optimism-is-a-strategy-for-making-a-better-future, accessed May 2, 2017.

18. Mary Helen Immordino-Yang, Joanna A. Christodoulou, and Vanessa Singh, "Rest Is Not Idleness: Implications of the Brain's Default Mode for Human Development and Education," *Perspectives on Psychological Sciences* 7, no. 4 (2012): 352–64.

19. Karl Alexander, Doris Entwisle, and Linda Olson, *The Long Shadow: Family Background, Disadvantaged Urban Youth, and the Transition to Adulthood* (New York: Russell Sage Foundation, 2014).

20. Nathan Kappan, "Race and Poverty in Baltimore," *Education Next* 15, no. 2 (2015), http://educationnext.org/race-and-poverty-in-baltimore-the-long-shadow -review/.

21. Elliot Eisner, "What the Arts Teach and How It Shows," in his *The Arts and the Creation of Mind* (New Haven, CT: Yale University Press, 2004), 70–92.

CHAPTER FOUR: "EVERYONE CAN GO TO COLLEGE"

1. David H. Freedman, "The War on Stupid People: American Society Increasingly Mistakes Intelligence for Human Worth," *Atlantic,* July/August 2016, https://www.theatlantic.com/magazine/archive/2016/07/the-war-on-stupid -people/485618/; and Michael Levenson, "3,200 Students on Vocational Education Wait Lists," *Boston Globe,* November 26, 2016.

2. James J. Kemple, *Career Academies: Long-Term Impacts on Work, Education, and Transitions to Adulthood* (New York: MDRC, 2008), http://www.mdrc.org /publication/career-academies-long-term-impacts-work-education-and-transitions -adulthood.

3. Catherine Gewertz, "Study Finds Little Tracking, Big Graduation Boost, in Career-Tech Focus" *High School and Beyond* (blog), *Education Week,* April 7, 2016, http://blogs.edweek.org/edweek/high_school_and_beyond/2016/04/study_finds _no_tracking_big_graduation_boost_in_career_tech_focus.html.

4. "President Obama Addresses Joint Session of Congress," *Washington Post,* February 24, 2009, http://www.washingtonpost.com/wp-srv/politics/documents /obama_address_022409.html.

5. "Don't Despair, There Is a College for Everyone," *College Parents of America* (blog), October 21, 2016, http://collegeparents.org/2016/10/21/dont-despair -there-is-a-college-for-everyone-2016-update/.

6. Ibid.

7. School and District Profiles, Massachusetts Department of Elementary and Secondary Education, http://profiles.doe.mass.edu/, accessed May 2, 2017.

8. Katherine S. Newman and Hella Winston, "Straight from High School to a Career," *New York Times,* April 15, 2016, https://www.nytimes.com/2016/04/15 /opinion/straight-from-high-school-to-a-career.html?_r=0.

9. National Skills Coalition, "Middle-Skill Jobs," fact sheet, http://www .nationalskillscoalition.org/resources/publications/file/middle-skill-fact-sheets -2014/NSC-United-States-MiddleSkillFS-2014.pdf.

10. Gilberto Q. Conchas and Luis F. Rodriquez, *Small Schools and Urban Youth: Using the Power of School Culture to Engage Students* (Thousand Oaks, CA: Corwin Press, 2008).

11. Andrew Sum et al., *The Plummeting Labor Market: Fortunes of Teens and Young Adults* (Washington, DC: Brookings Institution, 2014).

12. BAA's current headmaster, Anne Clark, has made it a top priority to ensure that the school can expand its CTE programs. Recently, the school was accredited for a vocational program in design and visual communications. I hope and suspect other vocational programs are around the corner.

13. Levenson, "3,200 Students on Vocational Education Wait Lists."

14. When my own infant son had to have a spinal tap, one of the phlebotomists was a Fenway graduate. I felt immediate relief seeing her there, since I knew she had had excellent training.

15. School and District Profiles, Massachusetts Department of Elementary and Secondary Education, http://profiles.doe.mass.edu.

16. Nancy Hoffman, *Let's Get Real: Deeper Learning and the Power of the Workplace* (Boston: Jobs for the Future, 2015).

17. Ibid., 10.

18. Ibid., 11.

19. Ibid.

20. Kirk Carapezza and Mallory Noe-Payne, "'Blue-Collar Aristocrats' Thrive in German Economy," *Marketplace*, April 7, 2015, http://www.marketplace.org /2015/04/07/education/learning-curve/blue-collar-aristocrats-thrive-german -economy.

21. Tom Birmingham, "Reasons for Success of Vocational-Technical Schools: Guest Viewpoint," July 2, 2015, MassLive.com, http://www.masslive.com/opinion /index.ssf/2015/07/reasons_for_success_of_vocatio.html.

22. Ibid.

23. Ibid.

24. Worcester Technical High School website, http://techhigh.us/, accessed May 2, 2017.

25. Hoffman, *Let's Get Real.*

CHAPTER FIVE: "IF YOU BELIEVE, YOUR DREAMS WILL COME TRUE"

1. "Action research" is a disciplined process of inquiry conducted *by* and *for* those taking the action. The primary reason for engaging in action research is to assist the "actor" in improving and/or refining his or her actions.

2. Mark A. Bautista et al., "Participatory Action Research and City Youth: Methodological Insights from the Council of Youth Research," *Teachers College Record* 115, no. 10 (2013).

3. Paulo Freire, *Pedagogy of the Oppressed* (New York: Seabury Press, 1970).

4. Social Justice High's Fire Project (Chicago), http://www.sojofireproject.org /overview.html.

5. Nellie Androveza, "'Distefano': Diane Guerrero to Star in CBS Comedy Pilot from 'HIMYM' Creators," *Deadline*, February 14, 2017, http://deadline.com /2017/02/distefano-diane-guerrero-cast-cbs-comedy-pilot-himym-creators -1201911871/.

CONCLUSION

1. Anemona Hartocollis, "College Is the Goal. The Problem? Getting There," *New York Times,* March 24, 2017, https://www.nytimes.com/2017/03/24/us /topeka-college-acceptance-applying-selection.html?_r=0.